T0317923

A FIELD GUIDE TO

BEING
BRITISH

A FIELD GUIDE TO

BEING
BRITISH

Edited by Tom Whiteley

Michael O'Mara Books Limited

First published in Great Britain in 2024 by
Michael O'Mara Books Limited
9 Lion Yard
Tremadoc Road
London SW4 7NQ

A CIP catalogue record for this book is available from the British
Library.

This product is made of material from well-managed, FSC®-certified
forests and other controlled sources. The manufacturing processes
conform to the environmental regulations of the country of origin.

ISBN: 978-1-78929-709-6 in hardback print format
ISBN: 978-1-78929-710-2 in ebook format

1 2 3 4 5 6 7 8 9 10

Cover design by Claire Cater, using illustrations by The Daily Mash
Designed and typeset by Julyan Bayes
Printed and bound by CPI Group (UK) Ltd, Croydon, CR0 4YY

www.mombooks.com

Contents

Introduction

IN BRITAIN, everyone knows their place. And, to ensure they never leave their allotted slot in the class hierarchy, they abhor both those who imagine themselves better than them above and those they're effortlessly superior to below.

But are the upper classes really venal fops who think only of titles and money? Are the middle classes really as petty and pathetically status-obsessed as they appear? Are the working classes really all white-van drivers consumed by Ginsters pasties, Ralph Lauren polo shirts and 36DD bosoms?

The answer to all three questions, obviously, is 'yes'. However, being British, we're able to laugh at our own foibles and more importantly to laugh at all those other pricks.

Whether you're a member of Britain's monarchy, aristocracy and political class, a *Mail*-reading xenophobe terrified of immigrants or a *Guardian*-reading liberal terrified of Arts Council cuts, or whether you have a proper job and support a lower-league football team, this book is for you.

In this book, the Daily Mash, a British comedy institution since 2008, will rip the piss out of everyone no matter what class they are, mistakenly believe they are or wrongly aspire to be. This is frontline reporting on Britain: The Class Wars.

Posh woman clearly fancies her horse

Next husband to be a plumber, decides woman

The drug dealer's guide to going
out with a posh girl slumming it

Guardian Blind Date marred by working-class person

Six historical class-based sexual role play
scenarios for unimaginative British lovers

Man waiting for electrician to give him
love and approval his father never did

Lucy Honeychurch in *A Room with a View*: Seven posh girls
who wouldn't fancy you even if they weren't fictional

Have you married beneath yourself? Take our quiz

What are the bourgeois causes of your upcoming divorce

24 Tinder photos that mean your romance
would need to cross class barriers

How to pretend you fit in at your
rich boyfriend's parents' house

Woman would, if she's honest with
herself, shag that builder

Class and Relationships:

Love across
the barricades

LIKE ROMEO and Juliet, like Lancelot and Guinevere, like Professor Green and Millie Mackintosh, love can flourish across even the greatest divides. At least short term. Because it turns out, whether you're married to a man who orders Newcastle Brown Ale by shouting, 'Bottle of dog, mate' across a bar, or to a woman who worries what the neighbours will think if they see a takeaway being delivered, romance loses against class all the bloody time. Here we celebrate those relationships that thrive across class barriers while simultaneously mourning them because, let's face it, they'll never last.

Posh woman clearly fancies her horse

AN UPPER-CLASS woman is obviously in love with her horse, it has been confirmed.

Lady Susan Traherne is married to a human, but also likes to feed her horse Trinket sugar cubes while gently blowing into his big horse nostrils.

She said: 'It is absurd to suggest that I, a sane and balanced posh woman in a healthy marriage to a much older red-faced man who cares only for shooting and cheese, could have feelings for a horse. Even if he is large, muscular, unfailingly loyal and has the long, sensitive eyelashes of a poet.

'Anyway, I only keep Trinket because horseback is such a cheap and practical way to get to the village post office.'

Horse Trinket said: 'Just to be absolutely clear, I am a gelding. You know what that means, right?

'We have a normal, healthy horse-and-posh-woman relationship where she puts on incredibly tight trousers and sits on my back for no reason, then afterwards we go back to the stable and she cradles my huge horse head while feeding me hay and telling me her innermost secrets.

'Her husband Gerry is a total bastard, apparently.'

Next husband to be a plumber, decides woman

AFTER A decade of marriage to a corporate lawyer, a woman has decided her second husband will know his way around a bloody spanner.

Emma Muir's husband Nathan, while highly skilled at sitting in his home office pissing about on a MacBook, is unacceptably poor at any manual tasks from changing spotlight bulbs to fixing a leaking pipe.

She said: 'God bless Nathan. He paid for this house, but I think I'm ready to go up a level. It's time for a man who shows his arse crack at work.

'There comes a moment, call it early middle age, when you realise having stuff isn't as important as that stuff working. Nathan's only answer is clicking Buy It Now. I can do that. It's time to get a man in.

'I'm looking for someone with plumbing experience, able to put shelves up, not afraid of a heavy light fitting, enjoys weekends painting bedrooms and can dig out a bush, no problem. In return, I'm pretty MILFy over here.

'In the evenings I'll make him a cup of tea and chat about traffic – that's what they like – and then he can listen to Radio 1 and smoke while I get on with my business. It'll be a definite upgrade.'

Husband Nathan Muir said: 'Can you shut the door? I've got Teams calls.'

The drug dealer's guide to going out with a posh girl slumming it

WORRIED YOUR Roedean-educated girlfriend is only with you because you wholesale cocaine? Here's how to make your relationship work while avoiding gangland reprisals:

Class As are the perfect gift

Make use of your non-traditional career by regularly giving your paramour the gift of a gram or five. More original than boring old flowers and she won't be disappointed. And when you're already stressed out about a shipment being seized by Customs, you can't waste time poring over the Boden catalogue choosing a cardigan.

Don't let her influence your choice of dog

XL Bullies are standard in your profession but posh girls gravitate towards a breed they know, and that's Labradors. Unfortunately, a chocolate Lab won't be a huge deterrent to the police. At most you'll get a few extra stash-flushing seconds as the cops are unable to resist ruffling his fur and saying, 'Who's a good boy, then?'

Milk your background for all it's worth

Bad shit goes down on the street and your girlfriend enjoys hearing about it. Which is difficult when your 'ends' is merely deprived and miserable and a typical anecdote is: 'My neighbour's on antidepressants because she's bringing up three kids on benefits.' Rip off the odd *Top Boy* storyline to keep her titillated.

Don't be intimidated by her friends

With their cut-glass accents and titles, it's easy to feel out of place in your girlfriend's social circle. However, their degrees are in History of Art at best and more likely from the dunce's university, agricultural college. You're constantly calculating margins and switching between metric and imperial weights, you're brighter than any toff with a 2:2 in Maize.

Never listen to her business advice

For the upper crust, businesses are a hobby. They gravitate towards the wanky and unnecessary, like 'party consultant' or opening a Costa Rican street-food pop-up. Your customers are unmoved by a funky brand identity and would only use their loyalty cards to chop lines.

Keep your career alive

Like all dealers, you're making your money then getting out. Get real. Your relationship is based on the vicarious thrill of dating a dealer and pissing off her parents. You're like Mellors in *Lady Chatterley's Lover*, except she never says, 'Give me the democracy of touch, the resurrection of the body,' thank fuck.

Don't pry into her personal finances

It's best you don't know about your girlfriend's income. The sheer scale of her trust funds will leave you in shock at what she gets for being born while you have the hassle of burner phones, busts and taking a machete to work. Bring it up and you quickly won't have a girlfriend. Although her growing out of slumming it will soon take care of that.

Guardian Blind Date marred by working-class person

THE *GUARDIAN'S* latest Blind Date feature has been ruined by the inclusion of someone who is not a middle-class tosser.

New media developer Jeremy Carmichael was bitterly disappointed to be paired up with nurse Gemma Tonkins, who did not share his interest in indie cinema or being subsidised by your parents.

Carmichael said: 'The date started badly when I found out Gemma didn't have an obscure media job. I'm sure nursing is useful and everything, but I'd been hoping to meet someone who makes promotional webcasts for Hulu.

'She was perfectly articulate and quite attractive, but we don't have that much in common. She had no idea who Haruki Murakami is, and I don't think her parents own a boat or a cottage.

'I considered going for a kiss, but she had to rush off because her cat was ill. Romance isn't in the air, but we're going to meet up as friends. Gemma suggested October 2040.'

Guardian Lifestyle editor Charlotte Phelps said: 'This was a mistake on our part. Next time we'll make sure Jeremy meets someone who runs a small art gallery and won't shut up about restorative yoga.'

Six historical class-based sexual role play scenarios for unimaginative British lovers

LOVE LIFE flagging? Need to spice it up with a frisson of that truly forbidden fruit, sex between different social strata? These scenarios will engorge you.

Chimney sweep and lady of the house

Sooty footprints in the parlour really give the words 'You've been a dirty boy' a new erotic charge. He's got a selection of long, stiff brushes, you've got an aperture that's been neglected for far too long. He gets his muck everywhere, you demand compensation. Can be played Victorian or Edwardian. Dick Van Dyke accent optional.

Minor royal and paparazzi

She's wearing a dress, which is big news. You're photographing her, because you're parasitic scum who can't make a living without leeching off others. But your eyes meet and there's a spark of lust. Soon she's sneaked out of the premiere and you've lost the press pack and you're doing her from behind in the alleyway next to the bins. So taboo, so hot.

Serf and lord of the manor

The class system didn't start with the Industrial Revolution, so take a journey back to when owning a cheese put you one above the neighbours. She rolls in manure, he hasn't bathed in a year; one owns the land and the other diligently tills it. To be clear, the land in this scenario is his cock. Squalid, candlelit, knee-trembling, priest-outraging love.

Thatcher and Scargill

The winter of 1984 glowed with lust. The prime minister and the president of the National Union of Mineworkers played out their passions across the country. She calls him to Downing Street for a negotiated settlement and demands pithead as part of the deal. Fists aren't the only thing being pounded on the desk, and more than picket lines are being crossed. If you're too young to remember those days, watch a documentary on it to get you in the mood.

The officer and the infantryman

In the trenches of the Great War, lions were led by donkeys that were bloody well hung like them. Give love-making new-found tenderness and solemnity by pretending to be an Old Etonian officer and a salt-of-the-earth bicurious British Tommy, both about to go over the top. Slip your hand in his breeches, stroke his handlebar moustache and think of that summer in Shropshire with Gladys in 1912.

Posh and Becks

One is the handsome but a little bit catalogue model footballer. The other the Spice Girl, so hot they let her in the band even though she can't sing. One's a cockney wideboy, the other's an Essex girl whose dad drove a Roller. You meet at a charity football match and the minor class differences between you set your loins on fire. During wild rutting you promise each other to launch a fashion label, own a football club and give your children ridiculous names. And all your dreams come true.

Man waiting for electrician to give him love and approval his father never did

MEN HAVE confirmed they lurk awkwardly around the electrician working in their home in the hope he might love them and be proud of them.

Homeowners admitted they only offer endless cups of tea, small talk about Arsenal's all-time midfield and hints about their important jobs because they crave the approval they never got in childhood.

Tom Booker said: 'My wife hired Roy to install spotlights in our steam room. From the moment he walked in, gruff, monosyllabic, avoiding eye contact, I needed him to like me.

'I slipped into the mockney accent I hadn't used since school. I called him "mate" and "geezer" and referred to my wife as "her indoors". When he told me he needed to go up to the loft, I replied with a regrettable "Top banana."

'But it was all worth it when he said, "Pass me that screwdriver, son." I complied and offered to hold the bracket straight for him, and he gave a grunt of assent that did so much to heal my hurt.

'"Is that good, Dad – I mean, Mr Hobbs?" I asked and he told me it looked great and I was his special helper, which on reflection is an odd thing to say to a 48-year-old digital distribution manager. But nevertheless, I glowed with pride.

'I told him we had other jobs he could do if he could come back regularly, like checking the circuit breakers, playing catch in the garden or just putting a reassuring hand on my shoulder as we gaze into the sunset, but he's very busy this month.'

Lucy Honeychurch in *A Room with a View*: Seven posh girls who wouldn't fancy you even if they weren't fictional

THE CAREFREE hot toff girl engenders a special feeling in the hearts and groins of Britain's men, but even if they did exist, these ladies would not deign to even notice you.

Lucy Honeychurch, *A Room with a View*, 1908

The breakout role for Helena Bonham Carter as Lucy, constrained by the social mores of her time, engaged to Daniel Day-Lewis but not that into him so you could work around that. The bigger issue is that everyone in the Merchant Ivory universe is fucking loaded, so unless you can afford open-ended Italian holidays, Lucy's not bothered. Sorry.

Princess Diana of Themyscira, *All-Star Comics* #8, 1941

It's worth a brutally honest gaze in the mirror before fancying your chances with Wonder Woman. She could get with Superman, but she hasn't. Keep that in mind. Also, there's a mismatch of strength; one overenthusiastic game of swingball this summer and your shattered skull is in orbit. Be realistic and go for someone more attainable like Cher.

Padmé Amidala, *Star Wars: Episode III - Revenge of the Sith*, 2005

If there's anyone not over her ex, it's Padmé. Anakin Skywalker's killed the younglings, Force-choked her, left her alone to have twins and she's still like, 'Did Anakin call?' And when the answer's 'no', she dies. Even if there was a brief dating window in there, she'd spend it mooning over her special Jedi. Typical debutante, never able to move on.

Purdey, *The New Avengers*, 1976-77

Perpetually rebuffing the advances of Gareth Hunt despite resembling, with her bowl haircut, a freakishly tall young Aled Jones with tits, Purdey represents a popular stereotype of the posh girl: not interested in sex. Also, as a karate black belt, ballet dancer and expert markswoman, you'll have little in common because you do nothing but sit on your fat arse.

Cersei Lannister, *A Game of Thrones*, 1996

And another obstacle of loving the upper crust: their family. They're far too into them, often in an uncomfortably physical way, though Cersei takes it further than most by having an active sexual relationship with a brother who has sired all her children. Due to this, and not untypically of the posh family, they're very overprotective and you won't meet their standards.

Elizabeth Bellamy, *Upstairs, Downstairs*, 1971

An unbearably spoilt rich girl with a faddish interest in socialism, Elizabeth is essentially that girl you met at university. And, like that girl, after slumming it for a bit she'd revert to type, stop calling in for spliffs and sex and callously dump you for a banker. Or, as characters were wont to do in the show, die in a contrived historical way, like a Zeppelin crash.

Lara Croft, *Tomb Raider*, 1996

Many, many issues. If you're not the adventurous type you'll get bored of leaping between moving platforms in a Mayan temple every weekend. You'll always be suggesting spending time in Croft Manor while Lara's straight on a plane to China for the Dagger of Xian. Ultimately, like all posh girls, she's the main character and you're a brief supporting player. Two months after your breakup, she notices you've gone.

Have you married beneath yourself?

Take our quiz

You may have settled on your Mr Right, but have you downgraded a caste or two in doing so? Find out here.

Who earns the most?

A. He does. Gus has a high-flying career in the family business which he'll one day take over. I work part-time because it gets me out of the house, which is mortgage-free.

B. I do, but only because Gary's been out of work since Wilko went bust and his new career of streaming himself playing video games hasn't taken off. But it doesn't matter because we have each other so we're rich in our hearts.

What's his parents' house like?

A. Beautiful: three floors, six bedrooms and almost two acres of garden. Not that it has anything to do with the love I feel for him.

B. It's not a house, it's a flat – and being on the 12th floor it has terrific views right over the estate. The lift doesn't work but using the stairs keeps you fit. Very down-to-earth and so vibrant, with the upstairs neighbour blasting drum and bass at 2am.

What's his idea of a date night?

A. It's only got one Michelin star, but there's a little restaurant we love. Hiring a chauffeur means we can indulge in a few vintage wines. Which are worth the effort, even if the process of him tasting them and saying adjectives can be excruciatingly slow.

B. Spoons. As Gary always says, it's not where you're at but who you're with that matters. And you don't even have to leave your table to order because there's an app.

Who paid for your wedding?

A. His parents: they're very traditional and saw it as their duty, no matter how much I protested! They booked a country manor hotel for 200 people. I shudder to think of the cost but it was so special.

B. Half and half: half from me and half from my parents. We kept costs down by only inviting close family and doing it in a registry office. But it didn't matter, it was still wonderful. I cried on the day.

Where's your next holiday?

A. It's very fancy so I'm worried I won't fit in, but the Maldives. Three whole weeks with our own private balcony and beach. Also, I'm worried because he can be very boring.

B. A weekend in Bridlington in a little B&B near the seafront, which concerningly is also apparently a homeless hostel. It'll just be wonderful to spend some time together, though Gary has also invited two mates.

How did you score?

Mostly As. Congratulations! Your partner choice has lifted you several rungs up the social ladder. His parents are deeply disappointed he didn't do better for himself and have put money aside for your divorce.

Mostly Bs. You've sacrificed your social status for love, which is the reason your friends make excuses not to visit. It is assumed you've condemned yourself to life with an unemployable slob because he's hung like Red Rum. If only they knew.

What are the bourgeois causes of your upcoming divorce?

JUST AS your children are much cleverer than other people's, just misunderstood, so is your divorce. These are the superior reasons you're untying the knot ...

Adultery

Or 'extramarital liaison' or 'ethical non-monogamy' – nothing so cheap as an affair. More a classy, subscription-based way to meet high-net-worth individuals with similar emotional and sexual needs. It's criminal that 'acknowledging the strictures of conventional monogamy via open marriage to benefit both partners' can't be cited as a reason for divorce.

Although sleeping with the au pair or personal trainer is a hideous abuse of power now, so hands off the staff. Instead, you slept with a fellow student at your sculpture class, another parent dropping little Luther and Ophelia off at the Montessori nursery or had an irresistible *coup de foudre* at your writers' retreat in Sardinia.

Therapy

Lower down the class spectrum they have 'mates' at 'the pub'. You have your therapist, and enough time and cash to pick at nagging resentments like they're scabs. And in your safe space, wondering why you aren't enjoying the perfectly ordinary human experience of being blissfully happy all the time, you decide to blame your spouse.

Is he really the unendingly supportive soulmate you always imagined? Can she really be the one if she doesn't understand your passion for Mahler and can't speak Italian? Have meetings with a different professional in a well-appointed office, this time a lawyer, convinced that you'd get the house? Then it seems divorce is best for everyone.

Home renovation

Watching *Grand Designs* is a substitute for sex for the lower middles. Appearing on it is more appropriate for yourselves. But however satisfying a double-height atrium is in theory, you can only have so many arguments with your project manager before it becomes obvious to the whole construction team that you desperately need a shag.

Sublimate it all you can beneath your conviction that a freestanding bathtub with a view will complete you, go over budget like it's erotically thrilling and believe a marriage on the rocks will miraculously improve when you're surrounded by rubble. Put the finishing touches to the globigerina limestone counters and begin your next big project: divorce.

24 Tinder photos that mean your romance would need to cross class barriers

You can meet anyone on dating apps and find true love. But if the hottie you're swiping right on has shared any of the following photos, it's going to be very fucking *Saltburn*.

1. Relaxing in a stately home, which upon further inspection is in fact their family abode where they live full-time.

2. Hunting (fox/stag).

3. Fish hunting (fishing, but only if in colourful clothes and/or locations).

4. At a tech/finance conference, looking like they're enjoying it.

5. At a tech/finance conference, presenting.

6. Skiing.

7. Snowboarding.

8. Looking at all comfortable with snow and mountains.

9. At après ski with woman who looks oddly familiar and oh fuck, is that Pippa Middleton?

10. With family of such height they can only have obtained it by generations of inbreeding, overfeeding and never having a proper job.

11. Wearing a gilet in any scenario.

12. Wearing tweed in any scenario.

13. Wearing red trousers in any scenario.

14. Wearing a flat cap in any scenario, except if they are a genuine miner from the 1800s or at a *Peaky Blinders* night in a Derby pub.

15. Happily partaking in some unidentifiable, wanky Oxbridge ceremony with confetti and jokes in Latin.

16. With a high number of naturally blonde people.

17. With a horse, which they could introduce you to by name and sire.

18. On a horse, looking comfortable.

19. In extreme scenarios, participating in a polo match.

20. Wearing a tuxedo or ballgown without a hint of embarrassment.

21. In a box at the races.

22. In a box at the cricket.

23. In a box at the Teatro dell'Opera di Roma, taking a selfie while an aria is being sung.

24. Standing with the oldest man you have ever seen, who is later revealed to be 'Daddy'.

How to pretend you fit in at your rich boyfriend's parents' house

Dating a man considerably wealthier than he admitted on early dates? Invited to meet his parents and the house's drive is a mile long? Follow these tips to fit in:

1. Greet with a kiss on each cheek: left first, no hug. No tongues.

2. Clean shoes and fresh tweeds are gauche. Wear mud-caked old wellies and a Barbour that looks like a dog gave birth on it.

3. Brace yourself for the unrelenting scent of spaniel.

4. When you mention your surname, they'll enquire whether you're related to the 'Hertfordshire ones'. Nod vaguely.

5. Be aware that your boyfriend's father probably only speaks cricket.

6. Take nice wine - preferably a French red from 2018 - but don't expect to be poured a glass of it. You'll be given the Blossom Hill the last visitor brought.

7. Don't be overwhelmed by the oil paintings of ancestors lining the walls. They're the equivalent of family studio portraits in a new-build.

8. Don't expect great things of the canapés. The rich are cheap and adore chest freezers. They're bought in bulk from Iceland.

9. Vegetarian? Not today you're fucking not.

10. At dinner, don't just praise the cooking, praise the meat: your hosts likely shot the animal you're eating themselves. Possibly as long ago as 2004.

11. Under no circumstance should you use the word 'serviette', only 'napkin'. In general, try to avoid words altogether and get by on gestures.

12. If you run out of conversation, just mumble: 'Claret, the races, hedgerows, incest.' One of the four should spark things off.

13. You'll be invited to swim in the unheated outdoor pool. His parents will join you, and they will be naked.

14. Never, ever, ever talk about money, in any way, shape or hot-form investment strategy. You might as well expose your vulva.

15. In conversation, never refer to your 'mates', only your 'chums'.

16. If they ask, 'Do you ride? Do you shoot? Do you ski?' respond in the affirmative. Surely they're not hard skills to fake.

17. Wear layers as there'll be no central heating. Don't ask for another blanket. Instead, request an extra dog.

18. Don't expect a lavish breakfast. Stale cereal will be on the table in Tupperware containers. You will then be roped in to help fix the stable roof.

19. If you think they like you, they don't. If you think they don't like you, they don't. The nicer they are and the more they use the word 'darling', the more horrified by you they are.

Woman would, if she's honest with herself, shag that builder

A WOMAN idling at traffic lights by a building site has privately admitted that she would shag that one in the hi-vis.

Accountant Carolyn Ryan was driving through central Birmingham when she found herself, almost against her will, conceding that there is just something about a man with cement splashes up his trousers and no top that gets her motor running.

She says: 'I like a bookish sort of bloke, well-educated, who respects women and speaks at least two languages. Also, that thick brickie can get it whenever he wants.

'I know, I know, it's such a bloody cliché, but come on, look at the muscles on that bastard. It'd be like having a go on a bouncy castle. And there's something refreshing about a man who doesn't understand anything.

'We'd do it once before he'd washed or anything, then he could shower all the grime and filth off and we'd do it again. After that he could have a look at that loose slab on the patio.'

Builder Wayne Hayes said: 'Yep, I love a dirty posh bird, especially if she looks a bit like that Zara Phillips.

'Just kidding. I'm gay.'

Six ways it's cool to be poor,
according to people who aren't

Five wild, crazy, transgressive musical acts
who were nice middle-class boys really

White middle-class schoolchildren
conversing in roadman slang again

Is this dirty old tramp homeless or a
member of the landed gentry? A quiz

Family keen to stress they are only asset-rich

Scholarship children trotted out at Open
Day to perform like dancing monkeys

Six ways of showing you're still working
class when you're middle class

Bohemian household just dirty

Proudly working-class man isn't

Grammar school children source
Monster Munch on dark web

The carefree, happy life I would live if only
I were poor, by a senior brand manager

Everyone in squat has trust fund

Delusions of Penury:

Faking poverty

for cool reasons

IT ISN'T easy, having money. While it makes minor material differences - food, bills, houses, access to education and six-figure-earning careers - it often makes you a victim of reverse snobbery, which is the worst prejudice of all. Can the wealthy be blamed for trying to escape their circumstances? For attempting to win respect by concealing the BMW X1 in the driveway? For trying to live like common people, as Jarvis Cocker so thoughtfully invited them to do? Of course they can, the fancy fuckers. Here we look at their clumsy, fat-fingered striving to pretend they are one ounce as real as those who grew up with the incalculable blessings of a back yard and a second-hand Grifter.

Six ways it's cool to be poor, according to people who aren't

LOW INCOME? Grew up deprived? Didn't have any stuff? Congratulations, liberal society fetishises your origins and is ready to explain it was actually cool and fun ...

Poverty made you innovative

Unlike those bores who just bought the latest clothes and wore them, you had to be creative. Raiding charity shops, crafting hand-me-downs, doing your own tailoring - and now you dress so differently and thrillingly, according to a posh girl who doesn't think she's being patronising. 'Honestly, you're so lucky not having to keep up with trends,' she adds.

You really know the value of money

According to those who don't, it's such a fun quirk of your unconventionally poor upbringing that you fear spending money. Not wanting to spend £200 at a restaurant that calls three spoonfuls a main course is so individual, until you stop getting invited out by your colleagues because you're always bringing them down about how much stuff costs.

You're way retro

'Love the vibe,' says a guy you've brought back to your place when he comes across your vinyl collection, which you picked up when nobody cared about it and it was the only way to afford music. 'I didn't know this had been released on vinyl,' he says about the original first pressing of *Led Zeppelin II* you bought in a library sale.

You actually had a youth

All your contemporaries in your fancy job spent their childhoods at piano lessons, learning Japanese, kickboxing and street dancing, and that was before their private tuition. Meanwhile, you were being young! Climbing trees! Having such a marvellous time! You don't disabuse them that it was largely hanging around waiting for Mum to finish work.

You get to have your own opinions

The wrong opinion is social death in the right strata, yet you're so brave and uninhibited and say stuff like, 'I don't see why we even have a monarchy,' 'Quinoa tastes like shit' and, 'Have you ever even watched *EastEnders*?' Your colleagues really wish they could live like that, but their parents might stop paying their mortgage.

You're so much more motivated

You're lucky: you have to work because if you didn't, you'd be homeless. It's so much harder when there's no incentive because you know you're going to inherit. 'If I came from a broken home and a terraced house like you,' your boss says, 'I'm pretty sure I'd have made it as an artist.' Then passes you up for promotion for someone he was at school with.

Five wild, crazy, transgressive musical acts who were nice middle-class boys really

THEY TORE up the rulebooks, revolutionised music, left a trail of destruction behind them and had solid qualifications to fall back on if music failed to work out:

The Clash, active 1976-86

General rule: if you went to art school, you're not working class. And that's where this band of wild punk rebels formed, albeit Joe Strummer did attend in the Hellmouth of South Wales, Newport. Still, his dad worked for the Foreign Office, Mick Jones went a very nice grammar school, and to this day critics prefer them to nasty common Brexit-backing Johnny Rotten.

Iggy Pop, active 1967-ongoing

The Godfather of Punk, the originator of stage-diving who no longer rolls around in broken glass but still performs bare-chested, Iggy attended school in a nice Michigan suburb with the son of the president of Ford Motors. He has presented Sunday afternoons on 6 Music, offering an edgy alternative to Elaine Paige on Radio 2, since 2015.

Nick Cave, active 1977-ongoing

Renowned for his many years of heroin addiction, and for drawing pictures on walls in his own blood with a syringe, Nick's done ever so well to pull himself out of it. Though with parents who were a teacher and a librarian who sent him to boarding school and art school, he had those wonderfully solid foundations. Kylie was rough in comparison.

Genesis P-Orridge, active 1977-2009

Good old Genesis, of Throbbing Gristle, Psychic TV and prosecutions for obscenity, outraging the tabloids and having their Arts Council grant removed, fascinated with the occult and experimental surgery. You'd never guess they attended the private Solihull School and ran Sunday church classes, though in fairness they went to university in Hull.

Divine, active 1966-88

The pioneering drag queen who ate a dog turd on screen also had a thriving disco career working with Stock Aitken Waterman - and it all sprang from a solid affluent Baptist upbringing with parents who bought him his own beauty parlour in the hope he would settle down, stop dressing as a woman and not make films in which he ate dog turds. They were to be disappointed.

White middle-class schoolchildren conversing in roadman slang again

BRITAIN'S WHITE middle-class teenagers attending excellent schools are once again speaking like Jamaican roadmen.

The offspring of the privileged, all of whom are forecast to achieve top grades, slip effortlessly into their roadman identities each morning after long evenings of enunciating correctly.

Year 9 pupil Joshua Hudson, known on the streets as Active J, said: 'Man's gassed to be back. Weekend was bare dead being dragged around forests, learning shit.

'Mandem crew gonna be bustin' da drive-thru at lunchtime. Not had Maccy Ds for time, bruv. Been scrannin' nuffink but falafel and hummus at garden parties wiv the parents' golf gimps.'

Rebecca Edmonds, who the crew knows as Becks the X, agreed: 'Gyal had to go glampin' in da Hindonesian jungle. Me and my fam in a big tent – had to listen to them two parents do sex for two whole weeks. Was rrrrank, bruv!'

And Max 01, whose parents call him Oliver O'Connor, said: 'Wha'gwaan, cuz? Not peng being back in dis uniform clone drip ting! Had nitty harcheological dig trip, brushing pottery and shit, heducational. Trashed my Air Force, blud. Man so vexed.

'Nang be back flexin' wiv my mandem tho, innit. Them wasteman parents and their fake-arse life-shit ting been controlling man all summer, but now man's bustin' swag! Latin next period still. Aight?'

Is this dirty old tramp homeless or a member of the landed gentry? A quiz

He stands in front of you in soiled corduroys and a threadbare cardigan, grime in his wrinkles and redolent of booze. But is he a filthy vagrant or a titled aristocrat?

How did he arrive today?

A. In a Peugeot 405 with an oil leak, an overflowing ashtray and a nesting hen on the back seat, adding, 'I really shouldn't be driving this without a licence or that insurance thingummy.'

B. By bus, and he didn't buy a ticket. As the bus left, you could hear the driver contacting the depot to inform them seat E5 would need a chemical clean.

What is he drinking?

A. A lukewarm glass of red wine. Every three minutes.

B. A lukewarm glass of red wine. Every three minutes.

What is he wearing on his feet?

A. The most fucked pair of dress shoes you have ever seen in your life. The soles are flapping and the toes are crusted with fossilised manure. Perhaps they were once black.

B. Two trainers from two different manufacturers, in different sizes.

How does he smell?

A. Like the bins outside a Benidorm butcher's shop in August, of dried blood and ordure and smoke and filth, with a stench both tenacious and forceful.

B. Like the bins behind a Greggs on a wet day in November, of rot and shit and fags and damp, with a stench both oppressive and depressing.

What kind of dog does he have?

A. Impossible to tell. It could be three or four different breeds. It could be three or four different dogs.

B. An Irish Wolfhound.

How many words can you understand in each sentence?

A. One, and that's rounded up. He talks like he's got a gobful of marbles and every syllable brings a fresh torrent of spit.

B. Three, and they're all racist.

How did you score?

Mostly As. This man is as blue-blooded as an Avatar alien. Curtsey to your social superior and consider yourself blessed to have met him. Hope he tips you some land.

Mostly Bs. This man is a filthy old tramp. Feel free to place some pennies in his hat and go about your day.

Family keen to stress they are only asset-rich

A WEALTHY family has hastened to point out that while they may be millionaires on paper, they are in fact only rich in non-liquid assets.

Despite owning two homes and a thriving business, the Turner family firmly maintain they are no different to anyone else because all their money is tied up in trust funds, art and high-yield stocks.

Dad Joe Turner said: 'People hear I'm a millionaire and they think I've got cash falling out of my pockets. "Buy me a Bentley, then," they quip. But I'm actually cash poor.

'I'd say I've got, what, less than 50 grand in liquid funds and the only Bentley I've got to give you is my own - and I'm still paying for it! Once they realise that, the shine quickly wears off.

'A few bad years and I'd be sweating bullets wondering if my Amex Gold was going to get declined and if I'd have to cash in a pension. Our properly rich friends sneer at us, with our short-term bonds and land investments. We live hand-to-mouth compared to them.

'Sometimes I'm envious of my employees who just park their spare money in savings accounts, rather than publicly traded businesses. They've got it whenever they want it. They're freer than I am, in a way.'

He added: 'It's hard, becoming a corporation to avoid tax. You lose something of yourself.'

Scholarship children trotted out at Open Day to perform like dancing monkeys

THE HALF-DOZEN scholarship pupils at an exclusive private school are being pimped out in a display of virtue on an Open Day again.

Saint Charbel's Independent Day School in Buckingham-shire, locally known as Chuffs, is proudly showing off those students who would be too poor to attend the school if they had not passed an exam.

Headmistress Margaret Gerving explained: 'We take our charitable status very seriously, especially when hoodwinking rich, credulous parents that we are a centre of academic excellence.

'So, every year, we provide two bright but impoverished children with patronising places, giving our rich but thick children someone to look down on and guaranteeing us two Oxbridge entrants.

'They're just as much a part of the Chuffs community as anyone else, though they don't go on the skiing holidays. It's so wonderful they've overcome the adversity of not having £9,000 a term to spend simply by being so clever they could end up as a Chaser on ITV.'

Scholarship student Lucy Parry, aged 15, said: 'It's important to parents of prospective pupils that their children mix with poor kids while they pay extortionate fees to ensure their children aren't at school with poor kids.

'I smile prettily and explain politely how grateful I am to have this opportunity, referring to my widowed mother and council flat even though I live in a nice semi with Mum and Dad. Who is still alive.'

Six ways of showing you're still working class when you're middle class

HAVE YOU risen from humble origins to become part of the middle class? Do you need to remind people of that at every opportunity? Here's how:

Support a shit football team

The middle classes steal the authenticity from everything, but they're too terrified of failure to support a genuinely crap team. Make a show of your loyalty to Carlisle United, Swansea City or Northampton Town and they'll edge away as if it's catching.

Loudly extol the virtues of 'proper food'

While enjoying braised partridge with polenta at a friend's, repeatedly tell everyone it'll never live up to the mushy peas, cockles in vinegar or bacon oatcakes of your youth, while never eating that stuff and shovelling in fancy gastropub dinners two-handed.

Smoke after one drink

After no more than one pint, produce a packet of Silk Cut from nowhere and light up while offering them around to your horrified companions, shrugging your shoulders at any cancer risk because everyone used to smoke 40 a day and they were fine.

Be sickened at how you're spoiling your own children

Never miss an opportunity to stress how disgusted you are with the material advantages you yourself provide to your own children. 'Kills me how they're always plugged into these iPhones. I did two paper rounds for a year to buy a ZX Spectrum - 16K.'

Read the *Sun* for the sport

Yes, the *Guardian* has a sports section, but you can't fundamentally trust the views of anyone who only discovered darts watching it ironically at university. The *Sun* would never say that climate change is more important than Liverpool vs Chelsea, and rightly so.

Go on proper foreign holidays

None of this 'gîte in France' or 'farmhouse in Tuscany' bollocks for your family. Try three weeks in California, a week at a private beach in Jamaica or a hot-air balloon flight over the Serengeti. And you take them in term time.

Bohemian household just dirty

A HOUSEHOLD that describes itself as 'bohemian' just needs to tidy up and push the hoover round, guests have agreed.

Ceramic artist Isabel Ambrose tells anyone who enters the house that the family lives a bohemian lifestyle, which appears to mean that cereal bowls sit on piles of books for days without being washed up.

Friend Jasper Reynolds said: 'Bohemian means arty, eclectic, unconventional and apparently drifts of dog hair in every corner and a toilet tank without a lid on.

'I hate to sound like some kind of square, but is dusting really so incompatible with the creative temperament? Does being a freethinker necessarily mean dirty paint pots next to the kitchen sink for six months at a stretch?

'It is possible to smoke spliffs and also empty the ashtray. I know, I've seen it done.'

Nine-year-old Isiah Ambrose said: 'My mum says we're a bohemian household, so it doesn't matter if the cat litter tray is always full of mummified turds because I'm allowed to do drawing.

'When she's out, my sister and me have this game where we pretend to live somewhere nice.'

Proudly working-class man isn't

A MAN who makes a big deal of being a salt-of-the-earth grafter is the most middle-class wanker you could ever meet.

Self-proclaimed working-class hero Martin Bishop fulfils none of the necessary criteria for his socio-economic boast but nonetheless makes it frequently and without challenge.

Affecting a nondescriptly regional accent, the 45-year-old said: 'I'm from the proud yet modest streets of Chiswick, which everyone knows is the rough end of Hounslow.

'Growing up, I went to the worst prep school in the area and used to have to cycle there myself while my father toiled all hours in the hot, dangerous air-conditioning installation business. Owning the company, but still.

'At university my student loans were upwards of a grand a year, so I could barely scrape together the cash to get drunk every night for three years. All for a degree that barely got me a foothold in the coalface of the media industry.

'And I've still got the values I grew up with. I bought my Jaguar second-hand, I insist on a ten-day ski pass to eke more out of it, and I won't have a room in the house we're not using because it's wasteful. It's just the man I am.'

He added: 'My favourite film is *Kes*.'

Grammar school children source Monster Munch on dark web

A GROUP of out-of-control pupils at a selective school have been caught sourcing corn-based, artificially flavoured ultra-processed foods from the dark web. The 14-year-olds, all of whom are forecasted top GCSE grades, bought and consumed the snacks in direct opposition to their parents' beliefs and their school's ethos. It is feared several of them may not now get into their first-choice universities.

Headteacher Mary Fisher said: 'This illicit supply ring was uncovered when Year 9 student Reuben Slattery was hospitalised with Flamin' Hot trauma.

'An investigation unearthed a sophisticated network of students illegally sourcing grotesque snacks and dealing them on school premises. Roast Beef £5 a bag, Pickled Onion £15, and the brain-melting high of Flamin' Hot for £50.

'While we commend them for their enterprise, we cannot tolerate the possession or consumption of such vile proletarian contraband. All those who may have developed a dependency are being treated with Sea Salt Popchips.'

Gang leader Ryan Whittaker confessed: 'Through the tinted windows of our parents' SUVs, we saw the common kids sharing salty processed snacks on buses. The females looked at the males with desire. We wanted that.

'We hated our homemade, unseasoned baked-lentil discs and organic air-fried turnip hoops. We yearned to be like them: cool, with onion breath and stinking fingers.

'We wanted that greasy film in our mouths, to chomp on delicious foot-shaped snacks until our teeth were smoothed out with compacted starch. We wanted Monster Munch, and we were prepared to go any lengths to get them.'

The carefree, happy life I would live if only I were poor, by a senior brand manager

AS A sensible white-collar worker with an arts degree, I would do all these wonderful things if only I were poor:

Have a nice drunken fist fight

Blows don't really hurt if you're a manual worker next to a flat-roofed pub, between the bins and a burned-out Mondeo. You laugh them off. I can't break my hand punching Fat Gary in the jaw because I need to be able to use the trackpad on my MacBook Air to add notes to logo designs. But I dream of that raw, masculine excitement.

Spend all my money on drink and fags

Imagine that, swaggering into Bargain Booze and clearing the shelves of Foster's and Superkings. I wish I could, but the Range Rover Evoque is leased and the children have viola lessons. What a joy it would be to sack all that off and get shitfaced in front of ITV every night, watching whatever's on.

Only dress in sportswear

Suits are so uncomfortable, and even when I go out I have to wear an ironed shirt and stiff selvedge jeans. I'd love to roll into trackies, a football shirt and a pair of sliders and spend the morning vaping on the doorstep before heading to the bookies. Compared to explaining our KPIs to a graduate trainee called Jocasta, it sounds incredibly fulfilling.

Keep pigeons

Or whippets, or ferrets, or any other stereotypically working-class animal that's grey and status-free. We've got a Labradoodle with a permanently infected ear and a chinchilla. You can't put either of them down your trousers and 'go down to the pub'. You can't spend hours tending them in their sheds. You have to go inside and talk to your wife.

Use the garden as a garage and fly-tipping site

Living in a detached house within walking distance of a train station means you have a large garden and responsibility for its upkeep. I'm always planting iris bulbs and refilling the log store. I wish it was an overgrown jungle where I keep an uninsured car, a dog on a chain and a collection of broken wardrobes. How the other half live.

Not be a senior brand manager

If they're not working at Aldi or selling skunk, they're all on Universal Credit, right? I'd give anything to spend my days doing fuck all and I wouldn't miss the money if it meant I didn't have a boss called Oliver having a six-day breakdown about the size of a font on our latest pitch deck. Lucky dole-scrounging benefits scum. They don't know they're born.

Everyone in squat has trust fund

EVERY MEMBER of an urban squatting collective has a trust fund they have not mentioned to the others, it has emerged.

The group, who are squatting in a disused restaurant near Stokes Croft in Bristol, all individually stated they would have no issue discussing their inherited wealth with their housemates, but it has never come up.

Freddy 'Binbag' Newbolt, aged 25, said: 'Money and material possessions aren't where our heads are at. We talk about important stuff like the climate emergency.

'Do we have power? Yes, but don't assume that's paid for. We might be cleverly stealing it. Food? The community provides. Ocado deliveries could come from a food bank, they do those. Weed may well be obtained through a barter economy of skills.

'But that's irrelevant to our mission, which is to show that you can live outside capitalism's oppressive structures and challenge the carceral state. If we need a car for that, one turns up. We don't ask whose it is because it's not important.

'Yes, we see our parents, but only to deliver ultimatums to decolonise their land and stock holdings. This property we have every right to live in, because that's a human right, it definitely isn't owned by Marcus's dad. It's just that the police are afraid to take us on.'

He added: 'Sometimes members do leave for gap years, yes. The struggle is international.'

Britons still relying on class system for their personalities

Dreadful couple referring to 'their' butcher

Grown man calls mother 'Mummy'

Ordinary bloke in smart restaurant unflinchingly ordering pints

Film a hobby but television not, broadsheets confirm

Lobster can't believe he ended up in bloody Lidl

Couple unaccountably fail to paint wall grey or blue

Public school dickhead calls everyone by their surname

The five items in the wardrobe of a 19-year-old rugby-playing student twat

Personalised number plate not personalised enough to make sense

Not knowing what *Abigail's Party* is: the ironic signs you're lower middle class

Yes, it is painfully obvious you are only in business class due to an upgrade

Working-class family still trying to see point of Christmas walk

Upper-middle-class family makes middle-class family look like complete and utter scum

Six class signifiers you mention to your builder and how much they'll put the price up by

Most people now not really middle class

Six everyday situations surprisingly charged with class tension

Bullingdon, golf or working men's: which club is right for you?

Shoreditch cat gifts owner bird crafted from nuts

Gran to commit ritual suicide after visitors see toilet roll without crocheted cover

Man who bought pain au chocolat will be 'posh twat' forever

I thought everyone had a cleaner

How to reassure other parents you are just as comfortably off as them

Fresher absolutely loving his new accent

Nine innocuous topics and how to have a chip on your shoulder about them

Tiny Differences that Matter Hugely:

How to tell what class you are

IF YOU try to explain the British class system to an American, within four or five sentences you'll realise you sound fucking insane. Putting the milk in first? Leaving the television on while you eat? Saying 'loo' rather than 'toilet', or 'pudding' rather than 'dessert'? How can an entire culture be built on such minuscule variances in manners? It's no wonder they went for easy-to-understand racism with its simple colour-coding system. Nonetheless, being British means knowing those minute differences in every detail and always being ready to sneer at a neighbour for having a floral wrap on their wheelie bin, alongside these dead giveaways ...

Britons still relying on class system for their personalities

CLAIMS THAT Britain has multiple social classes have been greeted with relief from a nation of people too lazy to have individual characteristics.

Teacher Emma Bradford said: 'I'm more than happy to let my entire value system be decided by a set of arbitrary economic guidelines.

'Without a strong, detailed class system I'd have no reference points. I could end up watching *Antiques Roadshow* while drinking an Oasis, wearing a top hat and stroking a Staffordshire Bull Terrier.

'I'd start to question everything and soon wouldn't be able to distinguish a cat from a barn.'

The updated class system includes the 'technical middle class', who have plenty of money from cash-in-hand jobs but spend it at TGI Friday's, and 'emergent service workers', who are poor people who think they're it because they work in high-end shops.

Salesman Sam Collins said: 'Far from being an archaic load of cack, the class system is a handy ready-reckoner for how to behave.

'As a "new affluent worker", I understand now that I must drive a stupid little Mini car, own at least six cookbooks and do cocaine every other weekend.

'Without that knowledge I'd literally have to make myself up, using my personal thoughts and sensibilities, which would be horrible.'

Upper-middle-class family makes middle-class family look like complete and utter scum

AN AFFLUENT middle-class family has been humbled by meeting a family who casually drop ski lodges and ownership of multiple horses into conversation. Accountant Christopher Slade and his university lecturer wife Joanne were comfortable with their position in the class hierarchy, and describing themselves as 'comfortable', until meeting Richard Cavendish-Jones and wife Romilly at an unsettling dinner party.

Slade said: 'Our children are at grammar school because we moved to be in catchment. Their children are at Cheltenham Ladies' and Harrow. They're a cut above, with straw boaters and buggering fags.

'Defensively, I assumed they're one of those families who are effectively broke because all their income goes on stupid school fees. Apparently not. They went on safari in the summer and saw the big five animals from a hot air balloon.

'As the dinner wore on, it became apparent their middle-classness shits on our middle-classness from a great height. Richard rubbed it in with a casual mention of attending Bayreuth to see the *Ring* cycle. I hate him.

'A new Volvo SUV means nothing to a man who inherited a Jaguar XK140. The whole table rang with laughter when it was discovered their holiday cottage in St Ives literally looks down on ours. And between Ajax, Phoebe, Araminta and Erebus, I lost track of which were horses and which were children. Though I'm pretty sure you don't call a kid Tamarind.'

Romilly Cavendish-Jones said: 'Poverty is a blight on society. I'll send the Slades round some old jodhpurs and a snowboard. It's better than nothing.'

Dreadful couple referring to 'their' butcher

A MIDDLE-CLASS couple have informed their friends that they got the lamb for tonight's dinner from 'their' butcher.

Olivia and Rory Hannaford said they ordered the rack of lamb two weeks ago, paid for it last week and collected it today from their butcher, who they strongly imply did it as a special favour to them.

Olivia said: 'Clive knows us, you see. He knows what we like.

'He's not our only butcher – there's a wonderful man we see at the farmers' market who's secured some very special cuts for us – but Clive is our absolute favourite.

'And he's only five minutes' drive from our fishmonger! So convenient.'

Guest Sally Kramer said: '*Their* butcher? I'd like to see them call him that to his face.'

Six class signifiers you mention to your builder and how much they'll put the price up by

HE MAY be wearing the latest fashions from DeWalt, but your builder's class antenna is finely calibrated. Detecting any of these means a corresponding addition to the bill:

'Rooibos tea?' - £1,000

Your first mistake. Tea means tea, not any of that herbal shit. Herbs are for smoking during a tea break. By admitting you've got a library of exotic teas you're admitting you've got more money than you know what to do with. Your builder can help you out with that.

'Obviously my next car will be electric ...' - £3,500

'Ah, so that's *your* SUV on the drive? Not a company one? So, you can afford £55K, or £500 a month if you're leasing it. Duly noted,' thinks the builder, who you assume drives his filthy LDV van everywhere but has had a Lexus since before he moved out of his parents' house. If you'd upgraded to a Tesla, he'd charge you even more.

'Oh, ignore all that in the downstairs loo!' - £4,750

Like Emma Thompson, you're humble yet proud but also have a keen sense of irony, so while she keeps her Oscar in the loo you keep cuttings of your children's achievements in there. Your builder can read and to him, perusing while at stool, it seems they've achieved stuff that doesn't come cheap. Neither will he.

'Will they be long delivering the bricks? Only I'm afraid we have theatre tickets ...' - £6,250

As a self-employed business owner considering every cost option to bring in a job under budget and at profit, your builder doesn't waste pennies. He's long since weighed the options in the field of entertainment and concluded TV's the best value and the theatre is for twats with money to burn. And since you're burning it, he might as well have it.

'Sorry, I must go to my office; I'm meeting our Tokyo end.' - £9,000

The home office was already an automatic surcharge because it means you have more bedrooms than children. But taking meetings with Japan? You obviously have more tax-free cash stashed in Pacific Rim accounts than a Tory Cabinet minister. You can liquidate one of those, because he'll need the extra in cash.

'We were really hoping to get this done before Tuscany ...' - 30 per cent on the gross

'Ah, beautiful out there, innit? There's a quality to the light,' says the man with cement all over his jeans. 'You got a place?' Delighted at this common ground, you fill him in about the crumbling villa you bought and the terrible trouble you're having getting tiles in the right terracotta. He nods sympathetically, and now you're being ripped off in two countries.

Grown man calls mother 'Mummy'

A 38-YEAR-OLD father-of-three still boldly refers to his own mother as 'Mummy', friends have confirmed.

Julian Cook of St Albans appears not to have heard the news that casually addressing your mother using the same word you used when you were two years old is frowned upon and is not the least self-conscious about it.

Colleague Victoria Gillian said: 'His phone rang. He said, "Oh, it's Mummy." I gave a little fake laugh at the joke he was making. Then he said, "Hello, Mummy."

'If I insisted on keeping up a habit that's ripe for a pisstake even in the latter years of primary school, I'd at least have the social awareness to hide it. He doesn't even try. He says it so brazenly you're too taken aback to snigger.

'Is she "Mummy" to all her children? Is he raising his kids to call their mother "Mummy" their whole lives? Does he, as we all suspect, call his wife "Mummy" as well, or does the mother thing preclude that? Why are we all so afraid to ask?

'Frankly, I wish I had his levels of self-confidence. It's like he's made himself impervious to humiliation with one simple act. He even wears a signet ring on his pinkie with no sense of irony.'

Cook said: 'Why would I call her "Mum"? Urgh. I'm not from the regions.'

Most people now not really middle class

MOST PEOPLE in the UK are members of the not-really-middle-class class, research has revealed.

The Institute for Studies found that the burgeoning new class consisted mainly of deluded working-class people and less affluent privately educated people.

Professor Henry Brubaker said: 'Everyone thinks they're middle class if they've got a house of some description and their job doesn't involve carrying buckets of pig intestines around. This has led to the rise of what we call the "not-really-middle-class class": car-showroom salesmen or HR executives who go to work in a suit but still read a tabloid and don't like books unless it's something to do while you're getting a tan.

'Alternatively, they might be people who seem convincingly middle class but don't have any income. This is because they've made some incredibly stupid career decision like opening an organic food shop or setting up a film production company making Welsh-language romantic comedies.

'Whatever the case, they're not proper middle-class people like doctors or barristers. They're all much more desperate than that.'

Plant-hire manager Nick Walsh said: 'I'm definitely middle class because I've got a large garden.

'It's very much my private sanctuary, where I can just sit and think and watch Sky Sports by putting my enormous flatscreen telly in the window.'

Ordinary bloke in smart restaurant unflinchingly ordering pints

A WORKING man on a birthday meal out in a moderately upscale restaurant has unashamedly snubbed the wine list in favour of getting the beers in.

Dave Metcalf, aged 52, took a cursory glance at the proffered wine list before shouting up the Stellas while nodding knowingly at his fellow diners.

He said: 'I ordered two to get me started because I've been places like this before, and the service takes bloody ages.

'Wine? 32 quid for the cheapest bottle of red? They're taking the piss. You know where you are with a pint, and you've got something to wash your seared scallops down with.

'You come to these places and think you have to act a certain way, but what everyone forgets is the customer's always right. They're as happy to bring you a pint as a chilled Muscadel or whatever the fuck.

'Yeah, I'll have the dry-aged rib-eye. Does that come with fries? Frites? Never heard them called that. And another pint of Nelson Mandela, thanks.'

Fellow diner Francesca Johnson said: 'I'm sipping a glass of Syrah, the La Madinière. But being honest I could go a pint.'

Six everyday situations surprisingly charged with class tension

WE SUPPOSEDLY live in a classless society, so why does class tension come bubbling dangerously close to the surface during the most mundane events?

Supermarket deliveries

Should you feign interest in your driver's route and working hours, or does it sound patronising? Do they want this tedious conversation about onions you've stumbled into, or are they just humouring the pampered homeworker? All you wanted was some bog paper and cheese delivering, not a nerve-jangling journey through a social minefield.

Seeing a certain breed of dog

A 100 per cent accurate marker of social class. Labrador: white-collar professional. Alsatian: self-employed working class. Staffie: borderline underclass. Okay, it doesn't work with all dogs - for example, Dachshunds. Who buys those hairy, saveloy-shaped freaks is anyone's guess.

Getting into university

Not such a big deal these days, but it's an achievement - and one you were quite modest about as a teenager. Then your dickhead Uncle Dave said something like: 'Don't suppose you'll want to talk to us peasants any more.' At least he didn't blather on about the superiority of the University of Life, where, it appears, everyone graduates with a double first in Stupidity.

Visit by a dopey tradesman

Middle-class types agonise over looking down on the lower orders. All very well until someone genuinely gormless comes to fix your boiler. Then, on a freezing day, an ironic comment like, 'Think I'll do a bit of sunbathing later!' will be met with the frighteningly literal response, 'No, it's too cold, mate.' Hopefully it's not a big job, because the conversation won't get better.

Accidentally slagging off someone's choice of TV viewing

Certain TV shows are, shall we say, deliberately targeted at the less sophisticated viewer, such as *Love Island* or *Mrs Brown's Boys*. You'll unthinkingly slag them off only for someone to say, 'I think it's really good!' You'll then have to pathetically backtrack with, 'I mean, it's very good as broad-brush humour; it's all subjective when you think about it ...' and so on, sounding totally spineless, which indeed you are.

Relatives visiting

Certain working-class relatives have incredibly forthright views about any topic they refuse to research beyond tabloid headlines. So any family gathering becomes a game of avoiding the hot topic or being subjected to insightful arguments like, 'How can a man be a woman? A man's not a woman; he's a man.' The only positive is that Uncle Dave has gone strangely quiet about Brexit by now.

Film a hobby but television not, broadsheets confirm

THE UK's cultural elite have confirmed that cinema is a powerful medium and an intellectually demanding interest, while television is brain rot for mouth-breathers.

The distinction has been made after watchers of prestige television, who slump blank-eyed and slack-jawed in front of the idiot box watching glorified soap operas, deluded themselves they were equal to connoisseurs of serious Iranian films.

Financial Times film critic Joseph Patten said: 'Film, not films. Singular.

'Tell a potential employer, patron or lover your passion is film and you're a contemplative, erudite thinker with views on the oeuvres of Scorsese, Lean and Kurosawa. Say you like watching films and you're a halfwit drooling along to Jason Statham in *Meg 2: The Trench*.

'It may seem an arbitrary distinction, considering film, films and television are all screens showing people doing and saying things and occasionally there's nipples. But they're all very different, and TV is the worst.

'At its very basic level, anyone who leaves the house to go to a building and pay £9 to see moving images is at least trying. If the building bans popcorn and you have to read the dialogue because the talking is in foreign, then congratulations, you're a cineaste.

'Shall we meet somewhere and loudly discuss the later films of Cassavetes? Leave the pigs wallowing in their streaming filth.'

Bullingdon, golf or working men's:

which club is right for you?

You're off down the club, but which one? Make sure your choice is befitting your social position by answering these questions:

How do you feel about poor people?

A. Sympathetic to their plight. It must be awful having so little ambition or drive.

B. Compassionate and afraid. It would be better for everyone if they could be kept behind fences.

C. Can't stand the bastards. You wouldn't see them in here, we all work.

What's your drink of choice?

A. Champagne goes down nicely, especially from a debutante's shoe at 4am.

B. Gin and tonic with a twist of lemon, served at sunset on the terrace. Like in the British Raj? They knew how to live.

C. Bitter for me, a lager for the wife and a couple of WKDs for the kids.

Who is your father?

A. Lord Cottrell-Stephens, 17th Earl of Berkshire. But you already knew that.

B. Local magistrate Maxwell Hoffmann.

C. Terry.

Where do you work?

A. It's not work as such, more a calling to do good in public life. As an MP currently, but it's only a stepping stone to the Lords. I also employ my whole family and have a few casual consultancies with lobbyists.

B. Accountant. Self-made.

C. Fuck's it to do with you? Are you from the benefits? I earn my crust, mate, don't worry about that.

How do you feel about taxes?

A. They're essential for a fully functioning society. I personally don't pay them, because I have too much money and don't use any public services anyway, but for others.

B. Absolute fucking rip-off, pardon my French. There are a few ways around them, if you'd like to make an appointment.

C. I give a discount for cash-in-hand.

What kind of car do you drive?

A. A Mercedes? I haven't taken the wheel myself since that 2004 ban for driving into a bus queue.

B. A Volvo XC90. Jeremy Clarkson rated it highly in a *Sunday Times* review and that man doesn't lie.

C. A ten-year-old Transit with one headlight out.

What do you choose when dining out?

A. Oh, I don't know. Ask Gerard, the maître d' at Alain Ducasse. He knows better than I do.

B. We pop to the gastropub in the next village once a month for sirloin steaks. They do it bloody wonderfully there, though it costs.

C. Big Mac Meal. Two of them.

How did you spend your time during the Covid lockdowns?

A. On the family estate, brokering calls between PPE providers and the Ministry of Health, for which I received only nominal reward.

B. Stuck at home doing Zoom quizzes and jigsaws while the kids went mental on the trampoline. Drink got me through.

C. Oh, did you do lockdown? We're essential workers so we didn't have to bother. Caught Covid three times, mind.

How do you feel about pigs?

A. Phwoar.

B. I never visit M&S without picking up a bag of Percys! My wife says I'm addicted. Miserable bitch.

C. Very important. They're what separates us from the Muslims, mate. I begin every day with a bacon sandwich to make that point. .

Are you addicted to anything?

A. Privilege.

B. Wordle.

C. Cherry blast vapes.

How did you score?

Mostly As. The Bullingdon Club awaits. Your contempt for people and rules oozes out of every pore. It's a matter of time before you're leading the Tories incompetently.

Mostly Bs. Welcome to the golf club. It's an incredibly dull sport, but they do a nice buffet on competition days.

Mostly Cs. It's the working men's club for you. Bingo, darts, meat raffles, peeling wallpaper and racist comedians. It's like the 1970s, you'll love it.

Lobster can't believe he ended up in bloody Lidl

A LOBSTER is dismayed to have ended up in the frozen food section of Lidl, he has confirmed.

Marine crustacean John Cookman said that being hauled out of the sea then frozen to preserve his succulent flesh was bad enough, but at least he could have been sold in a classy shop.

He said: 'I was hoping for Fortnum & Mason or at least Harrods Food Hall. But here I am, in Swindon's second-largest Lidl, trapped in suspended animation as people with multiple chins ogle me and make vague grunting noises.

'The life of a lobster is short and unhappy, but at least you're reasonably confident of being eaten in a large tasteful house, washed down with fine wines.

'Dear God, someone's discussing whether they could re-sell me on eBay.'

Shoreditch cat gifts owner bird crafted from nuts

A CAT perfectly attuned to its owner's concerns over the environment and soulless mass production has crafted an ethical vegan gift for her.

While the majority of cats are predators who kill birds to bring home for their owners, two-year-old Totoro resides within a community of ethical hipsters in a trendy London suburb and has learned to adapt.

She said: 'Because all my natural instincts are patriarchal and violent, I repress them. But I still had the compulsion to reward my cohabiting humans with a gift.

'However, it would have been inhumane, barbaric and frankly imperialism to kill a bird or mouse, so I acted on my nurturing inclinations and crafted one from materials foraged from a nearby vegan falafel pop-up.

'The bird had a walnut head with an almond beak, a Brazil-nut breast, peanut-and-cacao tulle wings and daintily tinted green feet sculpted from pistachios. The constituent parts were glued together with agave syrup. It was a work of art.

'It took me three weeks to craft, then those greedy fuckers went and ate it. The next one's going on Etsy.'

Couple unaccountably fail to paint wall grey or blue

A COUPLE have sparked confusion and panic among acquaintances after failing to paint a wall either dark grey or gloomy blue.

Eschewing both Railings and Hague Blue from Farrow & Ball, Florence and Gabriel Edmonds have instead chosen a lovely pale cream that lights up their living room and is rumoured to be from B&Q.

Friend Justine said: 'A home is not a home until it looks like Oscar Wilde coughed his last there. At Flo and Gabe's, he'd be leaping out of bed telling jokes.

'The way to decorate a classy, modern home is a collection of dark, moody rooms lit by lurid pops of colour from mid-century sideboards upcycled using tips from an Instagram video. That's what we've all done.

'Instead, they've paid more attention to weird shit like how they want to "use the space" and "admitting natural light" than how it will look online. Not like a boutique hotel, I'll tell you that. They don't even have a rose-gold ceiling fixture or a viridian velvet sofa.'

Flo said: 'I shared a picture of our lovely, sunny front room on Facebook – it's Dulux, Lemon Tropics – and now no one will come round. They've called it an abomination.

'Justine says the walls have to be grey or blue. She said we've broken the rules and everyone's deleted us off WhatsApp. It's no more than we deserve.'

Gran to commit ritual suicide after visitors see toilet roll without crocheted cover

A GRANDMOTHER has decided suicide is the answer after guests in her home witnessed the scandalous sight of a naked toilet roll.

Spare rolls in Rosemary Thorne's bathroom are customarily concealed behind a hand-crocheted cover, but it was receiving its weekly wash when granddaughter Emily and her husband Rob popped round unexpectedly.

Thorne, aged 82, explained: 'Like a filthy sloven, I'd neglected to replace it with a spare, such as the flamenco dancer wearing a freakishly voluminous dress or the one like a bobble hat for someone with a cylindrical head.

'As a result, the Andrex was left brazenly exposed. I only realised when Emily came out of the littlest room after going for a tinkle. She was white and shaking, as if she'd just met the Devil himself.

'The good name of Thorne has been defiled and our honour can only be restored by my death. Do not weep for me. Have me buried in an unmarked grave.'

To expunge the shame, Thorne plans to ritually disembowel herself following tomorrow's *Countdown* using a pair of abnormally sharp dressmaking scissors common to her kind.

Emily said: 'One roll may be exposed, for necessity. But two? That's inexcusable. Nana Thorne is doing the right thing. It's sad, because we only popped round with a Soreen malt loaf.'

Public school dickhead calls everyone by their surname

A DICKHEAD who went to public school refers to everyone by their surname no matter how much they wish he would stop.

Marcus Webster, who refers to himself exclusively as 'Webster', refuses to use anyone's given name even when told to, repeatedly, by everyone he meets.

He said: 'Oi, Hargreaves! Fletcher's talking a load of cock about this night out not happening? Set him bloody straight.

'Yeah, Smithson, Ramsey and me are organising it, soon as the lockdown's over, and we've already invited Galley, Woodhouse and Radcliffe. It's going to be legendary.'

Friend Hannah Tomlinson said, 'Or John, Colin and Angela, as their friends call them. And as everyone else calls them. Apart from Marcus.

'I get that they do it at public school, even shite minor ones like he was at. But he hasn't been at school for 18 years and everyone out here hates it.'

Webster said: 'That Tomlinson moaning again? She's fucking hilarious. Her first name? Don't make me say it. It makes me feel weak.'

Man who bought pain au chocolat will be 'posh twat' forever

A ROTHERHAM man who dared order a pain au chocolat, pronouncing it correctly, in front of his mates has been forever branded a posh twat.

Gareth Taylor, aged 23, naively thought he could swap his usual full English for a delicious breakfast pastry without realising this marked him as a member of the bourgeoisie for life.

Gareth said: 'All I did was eat a food from immediately over the Channel, but I may as well have announced my house was made of solid gold bars and I'd hired a butler.

'Every time I see my friends it's brought up. They doff imaginary hats to me and call me "Choco Lord". I'm asked how the opera was or what Jacob Rees-Mogg's really like. It was a two-quid snack at a train station before an away game.

'I've had to hide the tzatziki in the fridge when they come round, and I cancelled a birthday trip to Bella Italia in case they thought that was a bit much. I don't know what foreign stuff is allowed. Curries, I think?'

Gareth's father Andrew said: 'When I was 18, my mates caught me watching that *Betty Blue* on Channel 4. They wouldn't listen that I only watched because it had tits in it. There was no way I could ever live it down. I left Middlesbrough and I've never gone back.'

The five items in the wardrobe of a 19-year-old rugby-playing student twat

ONE YEAR out from A Levels and already driving like a Land Rover-owning father of four? Only difference between you and you in 30 years a couple of inches of hairline? Wear these:

A quarter-zip fleece

A remarkably versatile item that can be worn for business, i.e. lectures, or pleasure, i.e. every other occasion in your uneventful life from enforcing a cleaning rota to laughing intimidatingly when girls walk past. Can be left on even in a packed, sweaty club, otherwise how would the ladies know what your initials are?

Biscuit-coloured chinos

The tighter the better. You didn't build up those thigh muscles to keep them hidden from the awaiting public, did you? An overdeveloped quadricep can and should be the star of any outfit once you've invested in pale trousers. Ask your father where he got his and go to the same source: your mother.

A rugby shirt you would never play rugby in

There are work rugby shirts and leisure rugby shirts. And this particular collared, highly impractical, long-sleeved cotton jersey is the latter. Wear around town as a statement of solidarity with the 14 boys who've seen your bare arse, or, for a bit of excitement, head off to a rival student union and start chanting there instead.

A light-blue dress shirt

Get prepared for that J. P. Morgan job early. Being comfortingly hemmed into a nice itchy, rigid shirt quells bothersome worries that you don't have a personality. And helps ease through this awkward transitional period between public school and Sandhurst when you're not being told what to do every second of the day.

A gilet

Preferably a Barbour, or a Schöffel if your family owns a ski lodge. Incredulously correct anyone gauche enough to call it a bodywarmer. Flex your arms, as if to imply they would shred any jacket sleeve foolish enough to try to contain them. Never admit you're cold.

I thought everyone had a cleaner

I SUPPORT social progress, justice and anti-authoritarianism, but I haven't got time for squirting Harpic down the loo – who has?

My important media job starts at 10am. There's hardly space in my schedule to think up the right moral values to impress people at dinner parties, which is why I'm not embarrassed that a foreign lady cleans my bog.

As an enlightened, progressive woman, I chat to the Ocado driver as an equal. I do the same with children and friends' dogs. But I can't do small talk, put the tiger prawns in the fridge and be expected to sling a hoover around like some sort of stylish domestic octopus.

Besides, my cleaner loves her job and said there are no objective grounds for preferring a particular culture's moral values. Or, as she put it, 'Miss Eleanor, in Bulgaria no problem.'

Plus, I give her £10 an hour cash, on the condition she works every minute of every hour and always gives the microwave a deep intensive clean.

But to those who call me a privileged hypocrite and mock my 'white women's tears', I say this: I genuinely thought everyone had a cleaner.

Personalised number plate not personalised enough to make sense

A NUMBER plate that cost its owner more than £1,000 is personalised, but not to a degree that anyone other than he understands.

Tom Logan bought the plate 'J52 LO4' for his Audi TT at auction this year and believes it makes him instantly identifiable and could never be the cause of widespread bafflement.

He said: 'What does it mean? Isn't it obvious? The 52 is for my age, which I will be in 2026, and the LO4 is "Log". As in Logan. The four is a G.

'The J? The J doesn't mean anything, that's just a J. Why does everyone always ask about the J? Ignore that and it's my age and name. Which is brilliant.'

Colleague Sean Bennett said: 'It's incomprehensible. Even when he explains it there's only a glancing resemblance. It makes as much sense as the plot of a Dan Brown book.

'My registration, on my 2011 Kia Sportage, by coincidence has SB in it. That's better than his without even trying. But he's so proud, as if having three characters that resemble three from his name when you squint a bit marks him out from the common herd.

'I mean we all knew it was Tom anyway, because it's a twat's car and he drives it like a twat. This just makes it confusing.'

How to reassure other parents you are just as comfortably off as them

CONCERN AT the grammar school's gates that you may openly shop at Asda? Are they understandably worried for their children? Let them relax by following this guide:

Own your car outright

Dropping off children in a giant SUV just screams 'leasing agreement'. Choose something mid-range, preferably electric, and drop in that you got a discount for cash. If this isn't possible, cycle everywhere with your children in a trailer like the Dutch do, and ostentatiously pity anyone who doesn't. They'll soon realise you're one of them.

Mention you gave birth in a nice hospital

You 'weren't sure about the demographic' at the urban teaching hospital half a mile away, so instead drove 20 miles to the leafy one in a nice neighbouring county. While crowning.

Serve exotic vegetables with pizza

Pizza is working class. Add carrot and baby tomatoes on the side and it becomes lower middle. To boost it all the way to upper, add an alien element your child's friends are sure to mention when they get home, like truffled artichoke hearts or mini peppers stuffed with feta. They won't eat it but it's sending all the right signals.

Complain about Ocado

They always come inconveniently early, just while you're doing a class on the Peloton, and the substitutions! There is a difference between kale and purple kale, you know! Makes clear you are not a member of the Lidl class and allows you to mention you're growing your own organic vegetables for next year once you get the greenhouse shipshape.

Humblebrag about work

Sorry, got to rush home because bloody Nathan's in bloody Singapore again, so there's nobody to let the cleaner in. Honestly, why can't the heads of international currency markets Zoom like everybody else?

Spellcheck your WhatsApps

Your messages must be impeccable. A message to a fellow mother is no place for a missed apostrophe or grammatical error. Any flaw in your email indicates that you went to a state school and thought a degree from a redbrick university was an achievement.

Mull over a second home

It's so hard to make big financial decisions like buying a holiday home in Abersoch, so go over the details of tax, Airbnbing it and your worries that the kids 'might get bored of going to the same place every holiday'. Drop in that you were all ready to purchase in La Rochelle before Brexit hit, and you count yourself as one of its victims.

Return lost possessions in rope-handled bags

Maisie forgot her cardigan? Send it back in a Fortnum & Mason bag left over from Christmas. Nothing says stealth wealth more than the casual disposal of a rope-handled bag.

Not knowing what *Abigail's Party* is: the ironic signs you're lower middle class

ARE YOU definitely middle class but not of its higher orders? Too uncultured to know your proper place? These are the deliciously ironic warning signs:

You're ignorant of *Abigail's Party*

The decent, educated middle class are haunted by Beverly, the nouveau hostess portrayed by Alison Steadman. When it comes up in conversation it becomes apparent that you think *Abigail's Party* is an actual event. Everyone will find it hilarious you're not intimately familiar with a *Play for Today* from 1977. You quite like the nude swan art.

Your status symbols highlight your middling status

A Ferrari in your drive is flash but impressive. Your status symbols are grindingly unexciting: a new Ford Kuga, a walk-in shower, a kitchen island. Nobody has ever been murdered in a fit of jealous rage after revealing they'd got an impressive amount of storage space for plates.

You call yourself middle class too often

Bona-fide middle-class people don't use the term except when laughing off a horribly bourgeois purchase, like a pizza oven or a garden office. You use the phrase unselfconsciously and frequently. It's very much a case of 'the lady doth protest too much', although obviously you're too culturally bereft to realise this is Shakespeare.

You own bad art

A triptych of sepia photographs of a beach, on canvas? A painfully obvious Monet? An Art Deco New York cityscape with the words 'New York' in case anyone is in any doubt? An elegant, timeless sculpture of an elephant in a waistcoat carrying an umbrella? God forbid, a framed reproduction of a Banksy? Horrifying.

You've got qualifications no one has heard of

Bachelor's, master's, PhDs: all acceptable. Your dubious managerial qualifications? That paid-for course with a title like 'Epsilon Insight 3.0' that was impossible to fail? Shameful. Not significantly more pointless than a BA in English Literature, but smoking weed in Christ Church Meadow while discussing *Sir Gawain and the Green Knight* is simply superior.

You use the word 'common'

It's all manners and language, and yours are wrong. This condescending term might accurately sum up a family gobbing on the pavement outside Farmfoods but must never be spoken. But you do, with a glow of pride at what you've left behind now you're a success with an electric garage door.

Fresher absolutely loving his new accent

AN 18-YEAR-OLD in his first term at university is delighted with his new accent, he has confirmed.

In the summer, Josh Gardner of Hythe was taken out to buy the new accent by his parents, who thought he would really suit something a little more Estuary.

He said: 'It's a little bit Essex – though not too much! – a little bit Northants, and just enough of my old Kent RP to provide the underpinning. I absolutely love it.

'We tried on a few in the shop and I admit I did fancy Yorkshire, but apparently there's a set of attitudes to go with it that I found rather too hard to pull off. Pride? Why would they be?

'My mum was very keen on West Country because she adores Russell Howard. Dad feared it would tip too easily into yokel and people would assume I'm thick, which given I'm at the University of Aberystwyth is a very real danger.

'But as soon as I tried this one on it fit perfectly. Goes great with a baseball cap and allows you to hint at all kinds of gangland affiliations. The girls think I'm gritty and dangerous. Innit? Aight?'

He added: 'Will I still use it at home? Goodness, no. I'll be hanging it up and giving it a well-deserved rest, like my support for Fulham FC and my grime playlist.'

Yes, it is painfully obvious you are only in business class due to an upgrade

WE CAN all see you. Squatting there, a sunhatted, cash-strapped loser, revelling in your upgrade to business class alongside us. We see you, taking your tawdry selfies.

If you want to fit in here with us superior mortals, behind our Prada sunglasses and copies of the *Financial Times*, stop. Stop trying to catch our eyes and share this moment. This isn't a special day for us. It's normal, it's ordinary, it's boring.

Stop looking smug as the economy passengers board the plane, reclining your seat to the horizontal position and whispering 'losers' as they trudge past with their knock-off Birkenstocks and home manicures. We think that too but are not so gauche as to say it.

Don't attempt to make friends with the crew. They hate your chit-chat in grating, regional accents - which even our Bose noise-cancelling headphones can't seem to block out - as much as we do. Just because you both live your lives coupon code to coupon code doesn't mean you're pals.

And please, give the in-flight entertainment a rest. The light from your screen is distracting us from important thoughts about China and the stock market and emailing our PAs to tell our children we won't be attending their birthday parties.

I don't suppose there's any point telling you not to get drunk. Free fizz refills are heaven to you. But do it quietly. We don't like to be reminded we're sharing air with someone who bought their holiday clothes from a big Sainsbury's.

No, nobody wants to clink glasses. Or link arms and sway as you sing along to the *Friends* theme tune. And they certainly don't want to play peekaboo through the curtain back to economy class. Here, I never travel without Xanax. Take two. And shut the fuck up.

Nine innocuous topics and how to have a chip on your shoulder about them

STRUGGLING TO shoehorn regional and class-based grievances into everyday conversation? There's always a way for your resentment to rear its righteous head ...

Unremarkable foodstuffs

Cuisine is international as a matter of course these days. Paella is no longer something you eat on holiday. Tesco sells coq au vin. Regardless, anything that isn't rationing-era British stodge angers you. A vein in your forehead should be visibly pulsing as you snarl, 'I'll stick with pie and chips, mate!' at a friend who dares order a Thai green curry.

Books

Some books are highbrow, some are by Lee Child, some are simply tools for living. Not to you. To you, they're boring, pretentious and an attempt to make you feel inferior. 'What's the point of reading made-up shite?' you say, as if everyone else is labouring under the delusion that Paul Atreides, Atticus Finch and the tiger who came to tea are real.

The South

South of Birmingham, England is one vast leafy suburb rammed with private schools and stockbrokers. Metropolitan elitists live lives of unparalleled luxury in Luton etc. Satisfying though this regional grudge is, it doesn't work if you ever go there. It's shitholes from coast to coast.

Fictional privileged children

When the morning rush hour's gruesome, who's to blame? Bloody yummy mummies taking their Tarquins and Henriettas on the school run, obviously. The imagination seethes at hordes of spoilt Horatios, Pandoras, Ruperts and Arabellas playing oboes while riding ponies. And laughing at you. Always laughing at you.

Attending university

In your head, a Sports Science degree at Loughborough is a cross between *Brideshead Revisited* and Hogwarts. Three years punting down the Isis with a young Helena Bonham Carter? Bastards. Comes as news to recent graduates who borrowed £45K for three years in Salford, mind.

Knowing stuff

You're not an idiot. But when you drop facts like '*Don Quixote* is the bestselling novel of all time. Bet you didn't think someone like me would know that, did you?' into chat, anyone who isn't a fan of exhausting, combative conversations learns to avoid you.

Having common sense

Anyone who thinks they're a clever bastard has zero common sense. That's definitive and not just bollocks. A&E departments are overflowing with PhDs who've put their fingers in light sockets or sawn through branches they're sitting on.

Sainsbury's

Obviously, you already hold views on Waitrose that class war would find extreme, but you also hold a grudge against

Sainsbury's. The mere mention of it sets you ranting like Robespierre, but with your bottomless hatred focused on Taste the Difference ready meals.

Anything fractionally superior to the most basic version

An infallible process to expand the range of your resentment. Thus Pizza Express becomes 'posh', Earl Grey tea is the worst kind of social climbing, holidaying in the Algarve is ludicrous when Skegness exists. Ends with you screaming, 'YOU CAN STICK YOUR HOITY-TOITY TIN OF ENGLISH BREAKFAST UP YOUR FUCKING ARSE, FAUNTLEROY!' at an HGV driver.

Working-class family still trying to see point of Christmas walk

A WORKING-CLASS family taken on a traditional Boxing Day walk are still struggling to work out why four days later.

The Robsons were invited to the detached five-bedroom residence of the Alderley family and after a pleasant lunch were surprised to find themselves forced to go on a lengthy trek.

Dad Mark Robson said: 'We were worried about going to over to the Alderleys because they're a bit posh, but the food was great and they had these fancy pigs-in-blankets that apparently they made themselves. Tesco does them, but each to their own.

'But then, just as I was ready to start drinking seriously, they announce we're all going out. Pub? No. Walk.

'So, we tramped through some woods in drizzle while they said, "Lovely and fresh!" and, 'Blowing away the cobwebs!" We were there three hours. What fucking cobwebs?

'You've got food in, you've got booze in, there's good stuff on telly. Surely that's a day to keep warm with your family around you even more than any other day? Isn't that what Christmas is about?'

Wife Jan agreed: 'I'd understand if they didn't have a nice house, but it's lovely. Why wouldn't you want to stay in it? What's wrong with them?'

Male students afraid to explore
sexuality join rugby club

The 15 things you must
own to be working class

Slag us all you like but
it's 11am and we're packed
again, by Wetherspoons

Pampas grass means swingers:
sex secrets of the suburbs

Deliciously Ella is a job: six
odd side effects of Britain's
obsession with posh girls

Middle-class family still in
wetsuits two weeks after holiday

The middle-class person's
guide to working-class people

Family of four lose dad to marathon

Builder's van suggests he's
setting off on the Crusades

Six rooms middle-class people
think they need in their houses

Rich family basically takes over pub

Poncey foodie stumped
by ingredients without
geographical references

Swimming pools and other money
pits: a guide for the nouveau riche

Woman in art gallery just
guessing how long to stand
in front of each painting

Bride and groom invite casual
acquaintances to evening punch-up

Middle-class family tanning
absolute fuck out of National
Trust membership

Mob of crazed bankers' wives
roaming Chelsea looking
for homes to remodel

Common people doing nasty,
horrid things in Magaluf

Man cuts down to one insanely
expensive new fad a month

Cyclists epitomise the very worst of
Britain's privileged, metropolitan
elite: a Lexus driver explains

Middle-class child in
gastropub orders off-menu

The six most middle-class
ways of exercising

French mountain
covered in arseholes

The privileged girl's easy route
to getting a plum media job

'Each Ginsters wrapper holds a
million memories': a plasterer talks
us through his van's dashboard

Posh boy furious father has
chosen him to be the family Tory

Middle-class family's
showing off enters 'getting
some chickens' phase

What football team you're allowed
to support: a working-class guide

If not for our quiet,
dutiful heroism, grouse
would have taken Britain

Northern Santa tells kids
they're getting nowt

The Strange Customs of Alien Tribes:

The food, sports
and hobbies
of other classes

ACROSS OUR small island, rival tribes regard each other with bafflement and distrust. How can polo be a sport? Why have a room if you're not putting a television in it? What satisfaction could possibly be taken from the films of Peter Greenaway? From the enduring mystery of why anyone would spend £25,000 a year for private school when you can get school for free, to the puzzling question of what senior compliance managers do all day, we are a nation unknowable to each other. Until this chapter, which clears up all possible confusion forever. If it fails to, try reading it again and paying attention this time.

Male students afraid to explore sexuality join rugby club

MALE STUDENTS unsure about their sexuality are experimenting in a traditional, socially sanctioned way by joining rugby clubs.

Students away from home for the first time are combining their secret desire to see other men naked and their open desire to be permanently intoxicated by immersing themselves in an environment where they can do both.

Will McKay of Pontypool said: 'It's not gay if it's part of a rugby club initiation ceremony. That's an ironclad rule.

'So all the naked grappling, all the humiliations, all the mutual masturbation and root vegetables shoved up arses? They actually make you more heterosexual than anyone playing football. While letting you, you know, see if you like it.'

Howard Brown of East Grinstead agreed: 'It doesn't matter whether you're from a small, sexually repressed Welsh village or an aristocratic family, you can dip your toes into the waters of your homosexuality here.

'My initiation was epic. I had to wear a nappy and crap myself, do the baby elephant walk through the quad, the milk challenge, the soggy biscuit and I got seven snooker balls up there. What a week.'

By the end of their first year, McKay was openly gay and thanked the team for their part in his journey, but the early morning practices were too much. Brown was the team's prop forward and lobbying for the initiation ceremony to include more urination.

The 15 things you must own

to be working class

How working class are you? These are the 15 household items you must have in your home, one point for each.

1. Samurai sword, hung above fireplace in case of return to Bushido law.

2. Android smartphone with Greggs rewards app on homepage.

3. Dog named after sportsperson or fictional sportsperson.

4. Fantastic array of expensive electronic toys that any middle-class child would kill to play with, ignored for football.

5. Digital picture frame showing slideshow of kids, other people's kids, cars, dog as above and mate's stag night, including nudity.

6. Books, but not making a big deal about it.

7. Televisions in ratio of 1:2 per room.

8. Hand-waxed gleaming Toyota Hilux pickup truck.

9. Paved front lawn so Toyota Hilux can be parked and admired directly outside window.

10. Oversized Sports Direct mug.

11. Both colours of sauce.

12. Ashtray.

13. Fancy ashtray for guests.

14. Dyson kept openly in hall, because there's no shame in being clean.

15. Two adult children, both driving £30,000 cars.

Lose one point for each of these middle-class accoutrements:

1. Old furniture.

2. Bread-maker.

3. Board game The Settlers of Catan.

4. Record player and vinyl collection.

5. Overachieving children desperately trying to earn their parents' love but never filling the emptiness inside.

How did you score?
15-10. You are the workingest working class, with the pride and body type of a Bulldog. Truly you are the salt of the earth, to the extent that your mere touch dehydrates things.

10-5. Middle working class, with aspirational tendencies. Your Tony Parsons books and occasional purchase of smoothies could lead you on a dark path to Middle England.

5-0. Always sucking up to the bosses and laughing at their golf jokes, you cross picket lines on a weekly basis and nobody will pass you the mic during karaoke.

Slag us all you like but it's 11am and we're packed again, by Wetherspoons

A PUNCHLINE to you, are we? Sneering at our clientele and our carpets and the distance to our toilets? Laugh all you want. It's not even midday and it's heaving in here.

We, and our 800 venues nationwide keeping all kinds of wonderful old buildings open and busy, are entirely comfortable in our own skin. You, personally, 'wouldn't be seen dead in here'? Allow us to repeat that in a 'boo-hoo' voice while rubbing away sarcastic tears.

The verdict of the people is that you can keep your fancy gastropubs. You can have your £23 celeriac, beetroot and wild mushroom Wellington. You can stick your ironic board games up your arse.

Turn up your nose, but Britain wants to stare silently into the middle distance while sinking pint after pint at unfeasibly low prices. If they want to look up, Sky Sports News is on. If they fancy a chicken madras or fish and chips, we've got them covered.

It's not rocket science and we greet every morning with a queue of drinkers to prove it even before you've sunk your first overpriced cappuccino of the day. And we sell those too.

If we bothered to put Premier League games on, sold vapes and took bets, the high street would cease to exist. It would be boarded up like a zombie movie. The whole nation would be sprawled at Sir Tim Martin's feet. We allow your world to exist as a kindness.

And we've seen you. Snooty little hypocrites sneaking into our airport pubs for a swift pint. Checking over your shoulder before you pop in at lunchtime. Hiding the app on your phone in a folder within a folder. You've drunk our surprisingly decent wine. You don't talk about Curry Club, but you've been. Don't think we haven't noticed because we fucking well have.

So slag away. Be that person who pulls a face at Wetherspoons. We'll still be here and we'll see you next time.

Pampas grass means swingers: sex secrets of the suburbs

THE BRITISH suburbs may seem a sexless desert of women in gardening kneepads and men washing cars, but they are actually red-hot pits of depravity. These are the signs:

Pampas grass

As everyone knows, a proudly waving clump of pampas grass outside a home unfailingly means the occupants are wife-swappers who hold Saturday orgies with other married couples at which they serve trays of nibbles. The friendly sway of the soft pampas fronds is a lure to the swingers' club within.

Converted garage

There's only one reason for a garage conversion: a sex den. One that's outfitted with stripper pole, love swing, hand-cranked three-dildo fuck machines and four mirrored walls. That's what they're doing in there. Never accept the loan of a drill. You don't know where it's been.

9pm Thursday night dogging

They've all got dogs and they all walk them religiously, but Thursday's when it happens. That's the day you'll see them all, young and old, heading to the picnic benches in the park for their weekly outdoor sex show. All standing round wanking frenziedly, then going home as if they're perfectly respectable and it never happens. But it does.

Every fourth house is an online brothel

The internet is swarming with OnlyFans housewives and they have to live somewhere. While the kids are at school, they're upstairs in panties, logged on to some bloke in Malaysia. Check the wifi as you go past. If it's the default router name, that's a sure sign.

'No Turning' sign in driveway

The centre of the street's LGBTQ activities. Turning in their driveway brings the homeowner out immediately, ready to perform any number of lustful acts, which is why they're furious when you drive away and bang angrily on the window whenever they see your car after that. Because they're gagging for suburban sex.

Deliciously Ella is a job: six odd side effects of Britain's obsession with posh girls

BRITAIN LOVES a posh girl, whether she's telling us how to eat or riding a dragon while slaughtering King's Landing. But our class fixation warps society in strange ways ...

Deliciously Ella is a job

Britain murders a staggering 2.2 million chickens a day, so let's drop the charade that we aspire to veganism. And while Ella Woodward is very lovely, that doesn't explain the appeal of her brand. It's the promise of a new, willowy vegan life so much healthier and more ethical than yours that gives her an undeserved career.

The *Four Weddings and a Funeral* premiere shaped a nation

Most of Britain's iconic moments are borrowed. Yes, Diana, but otherwise nobody remembers where they were when Port Stanley fell. But everyone remembers where they were when a beauty with a safety-pinned dress appeared at a film premiere alongside Hugh Grant and a national obsession was born. Those posh norks are our JFK being shot.

Made in Chelsea exists

Granted, Britain knocks back reality TV like cheap booze, but the main draw of Chelsea was Millie, Alexandra and Georgia, posh girls all, poised in cafés, wanking on about minor personal problems. That it's still going after 13 years proves we will watch them do nothing endlessly even if one of them is called Binky.

So, so many posh actresses

You can't escape privately educated thesps like Florence Pugh or Emily Blunt, niece of a Tory MP, or Emilia Clarke asserting she wasn't the cream of the crop at her private school. Even Phoebe Waller-Bridge's prominent role in that abortion of an Indiana Jones film hasn't stopped the enthusiasm. And when they play working class? That really gets us excited.

Nigella can make toast for money

On *Cook, Eat, Repeat*, Nigella shows us how to make 'twice-buttered toast'. Apparently, she's so hypnotically fascinating viewers will accept a recipe that is letting toast cool so the second application of butter doesn't melt. The BBC must have considered simply screening her sleeping off a big dinner.

The Princess of Hearts will never fade

Britain will never get over its unhealthy fixation with Lady Diana Spencer. The numerous affairs, the interviews, the doe eyes, the photo in front of the Taj Mahal. While simultaneously being happy to vilify her son for acting pretty much exactly as she did, because he is a ginger man. He's not a posh girl! He's not even called Harrers!

Middle-class family still in wetsuits two weeks after holiday

A MIDDLE-CLASS family who returned from Cornwall a fortnight ago are still all wearing wetsuits, friends have confirmed.

The Stewarts have been seen gardening, driving, shopping and visiting National Trust properties while uniformly clad in wetsuits and apparently have no plan to take them off.

Neighbour Helen Archer said: 'I saw them over the fence and said hello and over wandered Bronwyn, wearing a wetsuit while raking leaves as if that was perfectly normal.

'Behind her the kids were playing with a frisbee, wearing wetsuits, and as we chatted Nigel came home in his Audi A6, carrying his briefcase, wearing a wetsuit. I didn't say anything. I didn't want to look stupid. It wasn't even raining.'

Nigel Stewart said: 'Why are we still in wetsuits? Well, first, because other people hire them but we've bought ours. I think it's important everyone know that.

'Second, they let everyone know that we've actually had a bloody good beach holiday while being responsible enough to stay in Britain, and that we spent it doing expensive activities like surfing, coasteering and stand-up paddleboarding.

'Third, you can piss in them.'

The middle-class person's guide to working-class people

ARE YOU unsure how to interact with working-class people? Don't worry, here is a guide to their strange - and often frightening - ways.

What do working-class people like?

Mostly a form of interactive theatre known as 'football'. Unlike Chekhov or Mamet, it allows you to join in by shouting, 'WANKER!' or, if you are particularly passionate about the unfolding drama, hurling a £1 coin.

What language do working-class people speak?

It may sound like a foreign language, but listen closely and you'll realise it is a version of correct English but with odd grammatical constructions like, 'You what?'

Much like the French, they appreciate it if you attempt to master their tongue. The next time you meet a builder, say: 'Alright, mate? See the fucking Villa play the fucking Tottenham? Gor blimey, I'd like a pint of bitter and some tits.'

Are working-class people dangerous?

Yes and no. A certain type of hard working-class bloke is what is known as a 'bullshitter' and will shut the fuck up instantly if anyone says, 'No, I don't agree with that, I'm afraid.' However, others are very physically strong due to carrying spanners all day, so think twice before asking if their tattoo is ironic.

Where do working-class people live?

Traditionally, in a pokey council house with a whippet,

mother-in-law and parrot. However, due to getting a job and not poncing around expensively at university, many of them now have better houses than you, albeit with more shit solar lights of fairies.

Should I have sex with a working-class person?

Biologically you are compatible and may even produce offspring. But bear in mind that *Lady Chatterley's Lover* is a fanciful novel and not a scientific paper on working-class virility, so some of them may be disappointing in bed.

Am I working class myself?

No. If you are middle class, you are not working class 'because you go to work'. That does not make you working class, it makes you a twat.

Family of four lose dad to marathon

AN UNASSUMING family's world has been upended after the devastating news their father has signed up for a marathon.

The Manns of Birmingham are reeling after patriarch Tim revealed he will run 26.2 miles next summer and is consequently recusing himself from all upcoming familial commitments.

Eleanor Mann said: 'I should have suspected. He was running more and more, joining clubs, calling it "training". Even when he was at home he was never off Strava.

'And now, like every other man in his 40s without the courage to have an affair, he's running a marathon. Out all hours, bombarding me with tales of chafed nipples and the chance of a sub-three-hour time, boring me shitless and dumping me with the childcare.'

Tim said: 'This is a lifelong ambition, as of last year, and it's only ten months away, so I'm having to ramp things up.

'Yes, it means missing out on precious moments like bathtime, potty training and trips to the soft-play centre with my wonderful children, but once they see me cross the finish line they'll know all those sacrifices were worth it. And if they don't, I'll tell them.

'After that, I'm looking into ultra-triathlons. Although there is the very real possibility that within a month I'll fuck up my foot and never bother running again.'

Six rooms middle-class people think they need in their houses

MOST PEOPLE get by with just enough rooms for basic life activities. Not so the British middle classes, who need these unnecessary spaces to survive:

Utility room

They are nothing without a room dedicated to slightly dirty clothing. While others let laundry pile up then pop it in the machine, well-heeled families need a room solely devoted to a tumble dryer and a big sink. UNICEF warns that a middle-class child growing up without a utility room is technically living in extreme deprivation.

Pantry

The larder's posher relative, the pantry is a place to store food that cannot be stored in the kitchen or it may explode. The pantry is a reflection of these families' relentless desire to hoard tins of Italian things, and to keep kitchen cupboards useable they need a place to store aspirational foodstuffs that only a masochist would eat - for example, red quinoa.

Playroom

If you loved your children and valued the developmental importance of play, you too would have a room dedicated to it. It would also get rid of the Hot Wheels on the dining table and Nerf guns under the sofa. The middle classes are onto something here but fail to realise you can put the telly on, thus removing the need for play altogether.

Boot room

Not content to leave their shoes abandoned by the back door for the next person to trip over like normal families, middle-class families dedicate a room to them. And not even shoes – boots. Either hiking boots for country walks no one really enjoys, or Wellington boots for wading in ordure. They particularly love that it sounds like a room found in a National Trust property.

Snug

An extra living room of unread books and a piano only Dad can play, a bit, badly? You have a snug, aptly rhymed with 'smug'. Containing the comfy sofas and an Olympic-size TV, but obviously not called the TV room. If that was the name, you may as well replace the Labradoodle with a snarling Doberman and get your baby tattooed.

Garden office

Do you honestly expect these professionals to work from home in a non-work-dedicated space? How could they perform their managerial-creative role of questionable value to society at the kitchen table? Unthinkable. And without a garden office, where would the man of the house sleep after yet another vicious marital row caused by the stress of paying for these rooms?

Builder's van suggests he's setting off on the Crusades

A BUILDER'S Ford Transit is emblazoned with more patriotic Christian symbols than a 12th-century knight setting off to Jerusalem, onlookers have noted.

Roy Hobbs's white van has a St George's Cross flag flying from the driver's side window, a painted version on the bonnet and rear, and window stickers proclaiming 'For England', though it is not clear how his fervent patriotism relates to his loft conversions.

His personal attire typically includes an England football shirt with the Three Lions insignia of Richard I, the devout crusader king who came close to recapturing Jerusalem in 1192. Hobbs, however, works mainly in the mid-Essex area.

Hobbs said, 'I do feel a strong affinity with the crusaders. Installing a walk-in shower can be a gruelling, unending quest much like retaking Antioch from the Caliphate if Tile Giant keeps fucking your order up.

'I don't have quite the crusaders' devotion to Christianity, not as such, what with siring four kids out of wedlock, never going to church and thinking priests are paedos. But we have patriotism in common. Admittedly I tend to express it by drinking nine pints of Stella while watching England in the pub, but I can see the lads being up for an eight-month siege of Tripoli if Libya gets off its arse and builds an all-exclusive resort.'

Homeowner Donna Sheridan said: 'It's reassuring to know Roy is accredited by the Federation of Master Builders and also ready to fight off Saladin's mounted archers, should they advance on our three-bed semi in Braintree.'

Rich family basically takes over pub

A WEALTHY family have arrived at a country pub and effectively annexed half of it for their personal use.

Braying bellend Ed Fraser, his loud sinewy wife and awful children always occupy at least three tables, even if it means leaving bits of the *Sunday Times* strewn across furniture while they greet friends outside.

Fraser said: 'We do whatever the fuck we want when we go to the pub. Why not? Who'll stop us?

'Usually we chuck our coats in one corner of the room, our wellies in the middle of the floor and just let the dog do his dog stuff.

'Ideally we will have another wealthy knobhead family from London staying with us, so we can have a nauseating conversation about how property in the area is still bloody reasonable, whether you're looking to move down or just for a second home.

'Sometimes we send our children to the bar with drinks orders, then get in a massive strop when the staff refuse to serve them. As we see it, everybody works for us.'

Poncey foodie stumped by ingredients without geographical references

A MAN who considers himself a gourmet chef claims he cannot cook a meal because he has no idea where the cheese and ham came from.

Melodramatic culinary tosser Louis Morgan-Jones searched for information on which county his cheddar hailed from and where the pigs frolicked during their short but happy lives and came up unaccountably blank.

He said: 'How can I produce an authentic gastronomic experience under these constraints when all I know of the cheese is weight and nutritional percentages?

'What kind of cheddar? What county, what farm, what heritage breed of cow? What was their fodder? How was it matured? How will it crumble? How am I supposed to engage with this cheese when it gives me so little?

'And the same with the ham. How can I serve this when I don't know what it is? If it was Prosciutto Toscano and the cheese was Pecorino Toscano I'd know exactly how to prepare it and serve it with a glass of Le Pergole Torte 2020, once it had been allowed to breathe.

'But instead, I'm given ingredients so anonymised it's like they've been through a witness protection programme. I can't cook these. They're strangers to me.'

Wife Nikki said: 'So I'll have to make my own toastie, then.'

Swimming pools and other money pits: a guide for the nouveau riche

THINK YOU'D enjoy owning a boat? A horse? It all depends on your attitude to burning money, which each of these boils down to ...

Swimming pool

Ah, your own private pool, for laying down next to in summer, sipping cocktails before a couple of quick laps. But you live in Britain. So mainly it's dappled with rain but regardless needs endless cleaning, skimming, filtration, all the crap. You'll pay through the nose for it, and you think heating a house is expensive? Try 20,000 gallons of water.

Boat

Put a wooden construction in a body of water and what happens? It rots. To stop it doing so is a fuckton of constant, expensive effort. On top of that: sailing lessons, mooring fees, designer deck shoes and a captain's hat. Buy yourself a boat and you won't be nouveau riche for long. Still, there's always cocaine smuggling.

Horse

Keen to feed your cash into something that shits it out uselessly at the other end? Blow 20 grand on an industrial shredder. It'll be more rewarding than this. If you insist on pretending to be old money, buy a horse, stable, pasture, saddle, shoes, trainer and all the kit. Save some money for the vet, because horses are alive and go wrong in many, many ways. You'll end up cheering when it's shot.

A second home in France

How romantic: a bijou *gîte* in the Dordogne. Relaxed months sipping wine and gorging on cheese from the local *marché*. You soon find that empty rural buildings are invaded by mice, slowly collapse, and the French tax regime means *le gouvernement* effectively owns it. You could have had a caravan in Filey, you silly twat.

Classic car

Like a horse, a classic car looks fun and doesn't really work. A specialist mechanic will, on its first breakdown, explain that sourcing a new carburettor for a 1956 Vauxhall Velox is akin to finding the Holy Grail, but he's happy to try if you've got an endless supply of money. Even when it works, you'll look a try-hard idiot pulling up at the lights by Costa.

Shepherd's hut

Like David Cameron, you fancy retiring from the hustle and bustle to sit in rustic simplicity writing a book. Like him, after laying out thousands getting one with a wood burner, kitchenette and oak floor, you'll soon be bored as fuck. The hut will sit reproachfully, absorbing moisture, slowly falling to pieces. An eternal reminder you're not as good as a shepherd.

Woman in art gallery just guessing how long to stand in front of each painting

A WOMAN at an art exhibition admitted she does not know how long to stand in front of each picture and is having to guess.

Liz Chester visited an exhibition at Tate Britain but confessed she was unsure if she had looked at a picture long enough or if she had looked at it for too long.

She said: 'I mean, I've seen it pretty much straightaway. That's the thing with eyes. They're quick.

'I didn't want to seem ignorant by moving on too fast but I didn't want to look like I didn't get it by moving on too soon, so I tried to do two minutes on each but that's a long time to look at one thing if it's not a telly.'

She added: 'I realised I was subconsciously looking at the bigger pictures for longer and I'm pretty sure that's not how art works.'

Chester's friend Ruth Howells said: 'That's why I always get an audio guide. It blithers on about Expressionist brushstrokes or some shit, but it tells you exactly when to move on.'

Bride and groom invite casual acquaintances to evening punch-up

WORK COLLEAGUES and friends of friends have been invited to the evening fracas of a couple's wedding.

Grace Wood-Morris and Jordan Collins have issued invitations to their daytime wedding ceremony for close friends and family only, and also to the evening reception and 40-man drunken melee ending in mass imprisonment.

Wood-Morris said: 'It's so hard because the seeds for the violence will be sown at the actual ceremony, so we've got to invite enough people we hate. But then guests in the evening, at a hotel we found that hasn't heard of either of our families so took the booking, need to be able to grasp the causes of the conflict quickly so they can leap to violent conclusions.

'With that in mind, we've got my estranged dad coming with my new and angry stepfather, and for bridesmaids I've picked Nikki and Gina, who were both engaged to the same bloke who cheated on them with each other. And he's coming to the evening scrap.'

Collins said: 'The lads from work are always up for a ruck and there's a lot of bad blood from the stag, which should help things kick off, as should the three cans of Stella per person Lee's handing out from his van in the car park.

'It should become a mass brawl when the DJ puts on "Come On Eileen", and I reckon we'll be most of us inside for affray before the night's out. Front page of the local paper. Now that's a wedding.'

Middle-class family tanning absolute fuck out of National Trust membership

A FAMILY have spent the holidays giving their National Trust cards an absolute fucking hammering.

The Newton family, who have visited six National Trust properties in the last five days, have admitted they are ripping the complete piss and have no intention of stopping now.

Daniel Newton said: 'I'm surprised they haven't put a block on our cards, because we are going totally fucking hog-wild. Castles, stately homes, historic cottages ... we don't give a fuck, mate. If there's oak leaves on a brown sign, we're in, out, on to the next one.

'They must regret the day they ever made us members. Hundreds of pounds we've had off them and we don't even go the tearoom, so it's pure profit.

'King John's Hunting Lodge, two miles away? Don't mind if I fucking do.'

A National Trust spokesman said: 'Shit. Shit. Why didn't English Heritage tell us they'd already banned these freeloading arseholes?'

Mob of crazed bankers' wives roaming Chelsea looking for homes to remodel

RESIDENTS OF Chelsea have been warned to stay indoors with the curtains closed as a horde of financiers' spouses-turned-interior-designers seize the streets.

The women, deranged by wealth and boredom, have abandoned their loss-making boutiques and hit the leafy roads of Kensington and Chelsea with Pantone charts and catalogues of vintage fittings.

Inspector Norman Steele said: 'Their children are in daycare. Their husbands live at work. They have nothing to do but feed their delusions of design genius until their urge to turn a former candle works into statement apartments could be restrained no longer.

'If they see into your home, with its outdated Farrow & Ball colours and fixtures bought from mere shops, they'll kick down your doors and remodel it by force. Soon you'll be living under ironic antlers and Murano lights, facing a six-figure bill.'

Chelsea resident Jessica Bradley said: 'The au pair was putting the children to bed when we heard the roar of a convoy of luxury 4x4s outside. They parked atrociously and disgorged their shrieking, moneyed occupants. One Mercedes SUV was at 90 degrees to the kerb.

'One shouted through a megaphone that our kitchen island was a disgrace, our feature wall so 2010s and the bathtub wasn't even clawfoot. They tried to smash the door down, but none of them have applied force to objects in decades and they no longer remember how.

'We cowered in the panic room until they went away. Poor little Atticus needed his inhaler and an oat-milk babyccino just to calm down. I don't know how I'll send him to baby Mandarin tomorrow.'

Futures trader Denys Finch Hatton said: 'This interior design craze will pass. I'm grateful for anything that distracts my wife while I shag a 19-year-old Russian bird at the Savoy.'

Common people doing nasty, horrid things in Magaluf

BEASTLY COMMON people in Magaluf are simply horrid, it has been claimed.

The island is currently overrun with nasty, vulgar, working-class people who are either rutting, punching each other or jumping up and down to so-called grime music.

Sensible nice lady Abigail Hadfield said: 'It is horrible, just horrible. I feel sorry for the poor locals, who would probably rather be running small handicrafts shops than massive nightclubs with eight-figure turnovers.

'Look at them all, with their big necks and Ralph Lauren polo shirts. I'd recommend we don't let them back in the country except I need some manual labourers to build an extension on my house.'

The teeming mass of oiks will tonight descend on the Booty Palace nightclub for a performance by MC Squonky and DJ Beastface, or something dreadful like that. Then they will ride mopeds around, being frightening.

Dentist Phillip Bauer said: 'They seem to have this twisted idea of fun that involves getting drunk and having sex, rather than renting a farmhouse in Tuscany and quietly nibbling local cheese. The girls are fit, though.'

Man cuts down to one insanely expensive new fad a month

AN INVESTMENT banker has set himself a strict limit of one new hobby and the purchase of all associated equipment per month.

Barney Ware admitted that while he loves the thrill of plunging into a new world of obsession, somewhere between orchid cultivation and smoking his own meats he realised it had got out of hand.

He said: 'There's nothing better than immersing yourself. Reading the magazines, sourcing the equipment, learning the terminology and chatting on forums about brewing craft ale or ice-sculpting with like-minded people, usually men. Always men. But that does plateau out after a while, and I can move on quite quickly. For instance, buying a £1,500 microscope and seeing a fly's compound eye was amazing, but it pretty much peaked there.

'There's a 1977 Triumph Bonneville that's never getting restored, there's the potter's wheel, the loom, the three tropical fish tanks, the clay tandoor oven where I'm storing my graphite golf clubs. It is beginning to seem as if my hobby is hobbies.'

Girlfriend Daisy said: 'In the last year alone the basement's been a gym, a darkroom, a tequila distillery, a vivarium, a bonsai nursery, a recording studio, a podcast studio and a bazaar of erotic delight. It's insane.'

Ware agreed: 'I am a tad faddy. I've booked a Zen Buddhism retreat in the Hebrides, learning to temper my inner tiger's voracious appetite for hobbies down to one per month. Then I'll do something else.'

Cyclists epitomise the very worst of Britain's privileged, metropolitan elite: a Lexus driver explains

THE ROADS in this country are a lawless wasteland ruled by quinoa-munching liberals on bikes who force ordinary, decent people to brake.

Lexus driver Jake Campbell explains: 'The tyranny of the cyclist is near total. You can't hit 45 in a 30 zone without fear – fear one of them will come precariously pedalling out from a sideroad, child in a seat behind, brazenly daring you to hit them because if you do then you're the bad guy.

'When you're in a steel box and can easily kill them just by turning your wheel 20 degrees to the right, they hold all the cards. They've got you right where they want you. You're their slave.

'It's hard enough thinking of other people at any time, and especially when I'm driving. But the moment you see some idiot on a bike who'd be as happy in a ditch, you're forced to recognise their existence and slow down.

'I may have the heavier, costlier mode of transport, the necessary infrastructure and the political support. None of that matters when I don't have complete immunity from prosecution. The sheer injustice of it all is shattering.

'When I can't even send him into a hedge, there's no doubt who's truly in control. Who holds the whip when the Lycra Illuminati treat us all as serfs?

'They don't even like cycling. They only do it to prove the tedious political point that you can exercise outside, instead of paying £400 a month for a gym like a normal person.

'Just last week I saw one turn left on a red light. And when I did, I knew I was in Room 101 of George Orwell's book *Nineteen Eighty-Four*.'

Middle-class child in gastropub orders off-menu

A BRATTY middle-class child in a gastropub has ordered off-menu with the full approval of his dreadful parents, it has emerged.

Nine-year-old Stanley was shown the children's options at the Plough & Dragon in Norfolk but instead asked for three venison sausages with butter-braised cabbage and port-and-rosemary gravy.

Waiter Stephen Malley said: 'When they came in half an hour late from a country walk with their expensive outdoor gear and bloody Cockapoo, I instantly thought, "Here we fucking go."

'We're a simple country pub but we've built up a bit of a reputation for our kitchen over the last few years, so naturally we're a magnet for knobs. I tell you what, though, this lot were next-level.

'First the boy wants to sit at the big table for seven, but we were too busy. That got his tits up. Then I handed him the kids' menu and he looked at me like I'd thrown down a snotty napkin before saying, "Do you have venison sausage?"

'I said I could check with the kitchen, but he said, "Well, you're not going to check with the Chancellor of the Exchequer, are you?" His mum decided this merited a photo, including my red face, and his dad said, "You'll be on *Live at the Apollo* at this rate, Stan." He won't.

'And guess who came up to the bar two hours later with his dad's debit card to settle the tab? Oh yes, I shit you not.'

French mountain covered in arseholes

A FRENCH mountain is covered in snow and smug, excitable English arseholes, natives have confirmed.

Awful humans from south of Watford have gathered on the mountain to slide down it on vastly expensive sticks, creating what looks like a giant prick volcano.

French mountaineer Elodie Jerome said: 'I'm up to my summit in total shits.

'Wankers who think they're gnarly because they've spent 200 quid on a pair of goggles and strapped themselves to an ironing board.

'Red-cheeked, status-obsessed skiing dicks, quaffing champagne and boasting about their crypto investments.

'It's like I've started sweating cretins. At least I get some respite in the night when they all squeeze into the clubs, get on the gak and jump around to some awful Dua Lipa song mixed by a Dutchman who's dying inside.'

Jerome added: 'It never ends. A couple of months into spring and I'm crawling with angry dads on mountain bikes. I wish I was a hill or a cloud.'

The six most middle-class ways of exercising

NEED TO get fit, but not in a grubby proletarian working-with-your-hands way? Try these:

Bootcamp in the park

What could possibly be more middle class than taking a communal area for the leisure of all and commandeering it for your personal use? And deliciously, everyone knows the man shouting orders at you is actually your employee and you could stop him any time you wanted.

Cycling

Practical, A-to-B cycling is for poor people. Instead, ride a ten-grand bike around country lanes in a large group, holding up traffic for miles until you reach a village tea shoppe, where you loudly say you'd buy the local vicarage if it wasn't for your 'bloody commute'.

Wild swimming

Swimming pools, unless you own them, are municipal swamps thick with the detritus of pensioners and schoolchildren. Lakes and seas, by contrast, are pure, natural and perfect for you and your clean-eating body, which has regular glacier mud facials. Until you get Weil's disease.

Underwater weightlifting

Weights are a bit nightclub bouncer. Aquafit is what your granny does on Wednesday morning. But lifting weights underwater is just idiotic enough to be plausible and none of your peer group will have done it first.

Going running with your kids

A 5K is passé, but a 5K with your adorable children Clarence ('Claa') and Mabel ('Belly') in tow, keeping pace beautifully with you and your sweat-free partner? Family time and fitness time all in one? You'll be the envy of the course – and imagine that photo finish.

Outdoor spin class

As pointless as purple carrots, as gratuitous as a Canada Goose coat, as wasteful as a Waitrose big shop. Be the first on your WhatsApp SchoolRunners! group to do it, or curse your missed chance forever.

'Each Ginsters wrapper holds a million memories': a plasterer talks us through his van's dashboard

YOU THINK I haven't been cleaning out my van's dashboard? Nah, mate, this is the memory palace through which I roam. Let me talk you through it …

Ginsters wrappers

That one's Frankley. That's Newport Pagnell. That's Sandbach. Every one of these wrappers is redolent of a wonderful snatched 20 minutes at a motorway services: a tea, a piss, £20 in the fruities. Just stroking that greasy plastic sends me back there, like Proust. French geezer, wrote shit.

Monster cans

The magic of Monster is it comes in so many flavours you never get bored. Some days I'm Watermelon Reserve, others I'm Super Dry Nitro. Mercurial and ever-changeable, son. This one here in the camo can's Assault, and it takes me back to this landlord who was trying to fuck me about with the bill, so I picked up my mate Metal Macca and we went over there.

Old copies of the *Daily Star*

An historical archive. There are papers going back to when that lettuce was in charge, as well as match reports, transfer rumours that never paid off and fit birds in underwear. Tell you what, when I get rid of this bastard to claim it and a full set of brand-new power tools on insurance, I'll drive it into a peat bog and preserve it for future archaeologists.

Vape bottles

Smoking? We still in the fucking '90s? Tradesmen these days are health-conscious, so we're on the vapes. And like with the Monster there's a plethora of flavours, each evocative of being sat in traffic telling a job I'll have to leave it until Monday. And nicotine. They're especially evocative of nicotine.

Parking tickets

Yeah, won't lie, get a fair few of those. I had a bogus blue badge but turns out you're still not allowed to leave the van on any yellow lines you like, which takes the whole point out of being disabled for me. But each one of these transports me back to a time when I was young, carefree and illegally parked. I don't pay 'em, I've got a cloned number plate.

Probably some chicken

You'll have noticed it fucking mings in here. Leave it for a few days and it knocks you sick, honestly it does. Anyway, that's always chicken, so I reckon a half-eaten chicken bap fell down there when I had to brake hard because some Corsa came out of nowhere on the A34 and that's perfuming the whole van.

The privileged girl's easy route to getting a plum media job

BREAKING INTO the media is tough if your fanny doesn't come with a pedigree. Here, sex columnist Annabelle Catesby-Jones (BA Classics, Newnham, Cambs) explains how ...

Have a strong portfolio

When I was studying at Cambridge, I wrote a deeply felt first-person piece about having my bike stolen for the student newspaper. Well, an intern wrote it up from my tweets. Anyway, a prestigious publication like that really gives you a leg-up to summering at a newspaper where your godmother is features editor.

Don't be afraid of hard work

Be honest with yourself. Have you got the commitment to drill down into issues like internet dating trends with names like 'wombatting' that barely exist? Can you give up a weekend to visit a luxury spa for a thinly veiled advertorial? Can you pander to reactionary old bastards with stories like 'I'm 22 and went to transgender Glastonbury – and hated it!'

Be blonde and attractive

If middle-aged desk editors have a powerful desire to fuck you despite you being younger than their daughter, they'll decide their paper definitely needs a girl-about-town correspondent. Never underestimate the importance of midlife crises in a journalistic career.

Have a trust fund

Media pay is shockingly low until you've got your first book contract, by which time you'll be almost 24. Ensure you've got familial wealth. If your parents are, for example, a cleaner and a delivery driver, suggest they change careers to TV director and novelist. It'll pay off in the long run.

Have wonderful friends

All that investigative journalism stuff is so *All the President's Men*. In reality, have a gaggle of friends named Peony, Senna, Calla, Iolanthe, Zinnia and Phlox, ask them about their rich little problems and write them up as lifestyle articles with a soaring lack of self-awareness.

Live in London

There are media organisations in Manchester and Edinburgh, and I think that's very sweet. I couldn't live in either because of the language barrier. But if you're committed to a media job you have to be in London, so ask around your parents and their friends until you find a spare flat somewhere acceptable. Chelsea, Kensington, Camden at a push.

Network!

The media is a word-of-mouth industry, so you'll have to network. Look for points of commonality with your contacts – perhaps you all went to the same fee-paying school, perhaps you attended the same weddings, perhaps you've slept with the same Greek shipping heir. In my experience it takes less than a minute.

Have your finger on the pulse of the zeitgeist

All journalists ask, 'Why do people want to read this, and why do they want to read it now?' For me, the answer is, 'Because everyone I know is shallow, materialistic and upper middle class so I've written four articles in a row about moving to the Cotswolds.' I might enter 'Must-have fashion wellies for a shooting party' for the Pulitzer Prize.

Middle-class family's showing off enters 'getting some chickens' phase

A MIDDLE-CLASS family has got some chickens as part of their ongoing commitment to showing off.

Affluent conformists Sam and Louise Radcliffe already have a tasteful house in the country, where they work from home doing some morally dubious consultancy work that involves fleecing local authorities.

Having recently bought a large white Audi and sent their favourite child to private school, they have now purchased some chickens they don't really want.

Louise Radcliffe said: 'It's so amazing having the chickens – our youngest, Rudy, adores them and has a special name for the big one that I can't remember right now but it's very lovely.

'And you get delicious ethical eggs, sometimes half a dozen eggs a month, which is just brilliant really when all you have to do is feed and generally deal with a load of chickens every single day.'

Neighbour Ian Evans said: 'I give it a fortnight before the fox gets the chickens. And six months before the next recession gets the Radcliffes' shite country magazine lifestyle.'

Posh boy furious father has chosen him to be the family Tory

A SCION of wealth is furious that his father has earmarked him as a future Conservative prime minister while his siblings get top City jobs.

James Roberts, aged 14, returned home from Eton only to be called to the morning room and informed he will be entering politics and may even be required to reside in Downing Street for a period.

He said: 'This is so bloody unfair. I wanted to achieve something with my life.

'While my brothers are doing great things running hedge funds and brokerage firms, I'm going to be standing as an MP in filthy northern towns until I've "earned the right" to a safe seat, by which time I'll be almost 30. Then, once elected to office, I'll have to take humiliating Cabinet positions like justice secretary and work my way up, like a graduate from a redbrick, until I get a shot at prime minister. Which I'll have to be elected to. By *them*.

'After that I get ten years in charge, if I'm lucky enough to perform as well as a grocer's daughter or a Fettes boy, before spending the rest of my life giving tawdry speeches to new-money millionaires.

'And I'm sworn off cocaine, insider trading and siring bastards for the next half-century for this? The life of the well-bred truly is hell.'

What football team you're allowed to support: a working-class guide

YOU CAN'T just pick what team you support, son. That implies the allegiance that will govern your happiness for the rest of your life is arbitrary. Follow these rules:

Geography

The ground that's nearest your house? That's your team. Simple as. And it's crow flies as well, none of this, 'Well, if you take the A34' bollocks. Don't matter if you grew up in a penthouse apartment with a concierge in Canary Wharf because your dad's in high finance, you're a Millwall fan now. Deal with it.

Who your dad supports

Course, that rule's superseded by who your dad supports. That's how you're raised and nurture beats nature. Don't matter if you're two streets off Old Trafford, if he's drummed it in from being a kid then you're Rams until your dying day. Pity you, like, as they're a shower of shite. Can't see the Saudis coming in for them either.

Lower-league exemption clause

All that being said, you can't spend your whole life supporting Rushden and fucking Diamonds. You've got the right to a big club, and if you live in the middle of nowhere like that you're as near to Coventry as Luton as Leicester, so when you're a kid and your head was turned easy you can support whoever was big when you grew up. Even Chelsea.

But you stick with it

Once you've made that choice there's no going back, though. Born in Devon and fell for Leeds during their all-conquering Revie years? Then you're with them for the duration. It's nobody's fault but your own that you support a Championship side. Your payback for being a glory-hunting arsehole when you were eight.

And you're allowed a foreign one

This is like with the list of famous birds your wife would theoretically let you shag: it's not real but it's good for cheering you up when you're eating sandwiches in a Portakabin in the rain. So yeah, your Barcelonas, your Bayer Leverkusen, your Juventus, back 'em all you like. Not Real Madrid, though – come on, have some fucking imagination.

England

Or Scotland, if you're that way inclined, you poor bastard. Wales? Come on. You've got an English grandparent, we'll let you. Anyway, yeah, England's got to have your full backing at all times, by which I mean you've got to slag off the manager, hate half the side, and if you ever meet those pricks who play *The Great Escape*, God help them.

If not for our quiet, dutiful heroism, grouse would have taken Britain

WE DO not boast. We ask for neither medals nor garlands. Instead, each August 12th, the well-born shoulder their rifles and travel north to fight the grouse menace.

It does not matter who you are. Lords and Ladies, Baronesses and Viscounts, mere knights of the realm. We accept millionaires, even, no questions asked. Ceremony cannot be stood upon. We have no choice but to unite and stand firm because they are advancing, in their tens of thousands, with their russet plumage and that vicious comb of red over their eyes. From the Highlands they march. We are the only line of defence.

What of the Scottish? Oh, they nurture this threat by leaving their moorlands uninhabited. In their primitive, bestial way, it seems they feel it would wreak revenge on the English for their crime of being better.

What of the north, which would surely be the first to fall? I regret they are shamefully indifferent. I have never seen a wet nurse or a millworker line up in tweeds to bag a bird, much as they would be welcome.

So, it falls to us. The aristocracy. The last remnants of a greater England. Asking not garlands for our heroism, except the abolition of inheritance tax, we flush these grouse and shoot them down without mercy. Defending our king and our country.

Do we make a sport of it? Perhaps, but who would not? What soldier does not take delight in his marksmanship? But I swear that we do this not for the pleasure but to stop the grouse invasion. And come autumn, we turn our attention to fighting the foxes that threaten everything we hold dear. For ours is a life of selfless service.

Northern Santa tells kids they're getting nowt

A FATHER Christmas in Preston has informed children that they are getting 'sod all' because they have been 'bad little buggers'.

The Santa, whose grotto is in St George's shopping centre next to the disabled toilets, was exposed when a southern seven-year-old visiting relatives was given the choice of a 'clip round the ear' or 'shite in a bag' for his grotto gift.

Deborah England of Kingston upon Thames said: 'Archie went in all smiles, ready to ask for the virtual reality headset that he's decided he'd like this year. But he came out weeping, saying that Father Christmas had told him he was a "soft get", that his Christmas dinner would be "shit with sugar on", and that he'd be getting "nowt but a tangerine and be bloody glad for it".

'We've had to take our Christmas tree down. It brings on his PTSD.'

Brother-in-law Alan England of Preston said: 'So wait, down south Santa Claus gives kids presents they'd like and isn't allowed to use foul language or violence?

'Tragic. They're losing out on that marvellous moment when they find out he's not real.'

Middle class full, lower rungs told

Other cans think San Pellegrino is an arsehole

Council estate family intent on betterment have two washing machines on front lawn

Are you a common person being blanked at a posh garden party, or a ghost?

Living near a Waitrose makes you a 12 per cent better person

Downwardly mobile millennial hoping for working-class son

University of Life brings in tuition fees

Son of retired factory worker wishes people could tell

Oxbridge graduate or cocaine dealer: who's really got their shit together?

Social climber draws the line at opera

Striving family exchange TV too big for their living room for Aga too big for their kitchen

Man celebrates pay rise by choosing slightly more expensive version of everything for the rest of his life

You never got piano lessons as a child. Here's how to process your trauma

Upwardly mobile man despised by those above, those below and his peers

Working classes 'must express themselves only through National Theatre productions'

Successful man urged always to remember shite childhood of poverty

Broken espresso machine temporarily demotes family down a social class

No progress on Essex prime minister

Eliza Doolittle a 'filthy class traitor'

Aspirational woman orders first set of beef cheeks

This week in Mash History: steerage passengers on *Titanic* struggle to surmount class barriers, 1912

Meritocracy no use if you're thick, complain cretins

Friend with wife, children and six-figure job thinks he's better than you

Feeling Ashamed of Your Parents in Restaurants:

Social climbing for fun and profit

BRITAIN WOULDN'T be Britain without the myth of betterment. Without the belief that you can, through hard work and talent, move up a social class and be accepted. It is, of course, bollocks. Apart from odd exceptions like Bryan Ferry and Holly Valance, both of whom ascended by shagging, all you'll climb to is a world of sneers, snide remarks and backbiting. You'll conclude it was not remotely worth the effort, which it incidentally has in common with any mountain. Still, given that your children are already a higher class than you and chuckle behind their hands when you order in restaurants, it's too late now. Stuck-up little bastards.

Middle class full, lower rungs told

THE LOWER stratas of society have been informed that the middle class is now completely full so they should stop trying to get in.

Plebs, chavs and benefits claimants have been firmly advised there are no vacancies in society's cushy median layer, so they should pack up their pathetic aspirations and learn to enjoy whichever subterranean bracket they were born into.

Social analyst Dylan French said: 'A homebirth baby snapped up the last middle-class slot at 7.04 this morning. So until a lawyer dies or a solicitor emigrates, you can't come in.

'We're crammed in here like a North Face cagoule stuffed into a Kånken backpack. Oh, cagoule is a fancy name for a raincoat, from the French word for "cowl". You don't speak French? Well, you see.

'Don't trespass on our hallowed domain by reading the *Guardian* or sticking a conservatory onto your terraced house, it won't make a difference. You'll only be robbing your betters of pithy Owen Jones columns that will go right over your head.

'Besides, why would you want to be middle class? It's mainly just going on hikes and drinking oat milk. You surely have much more fun dancing Irish jigs in your boiler room and playing tin whistles or whatever it is you get up to.

'Anyway, that's you told nicely. Don't make us give the army the fire order.'

Other cans think San Pellegrino is an arsehole

ALL OTHER canned drinks regard San Pellegrino as a smug prick with a stupid foil hat, it has emerged.

Coke can Lee Higgs of Sonni's News, Islington, said: 'We've got a San Pellegrino can in our fridge and, trust me, you'd be hard-pressed to find a bigger dickhead.

'You can tell he thinks he's better than the rest of us, just because he's got a fancy foreign name and he's 22p more expensive. I tried to chat to him once, but he just turned his back on me and started talking to the Perrier bottles about some fucking BBC4 thing he'd seen.'

Sprite can Steve Macdonald said: 'I remember when he first showed up with that fucking foil hat on. I said to the Fanta, "That thing's going out the door first chance I get." But then, when I tried to grab it off him, he started crying and saying how his ring-pull would get all rusty without it.

'He's such a twat, honestly.'

Lilt can Angie Adams said: 'We all call him Wicksy, because his little foil hat is like the one mad Joe Wicks used to wear in *EastEnders*.

'He just sneers at us and says he's never seen *EastEnders*, but you can tell it gets to him.'

Council estate family intent on betterment have two washing machines on front lawn

A FAMILY keen to show they are a notch above their neighbours have not one but two disused washing machines in their garden.

The Hursts have one-upped other residents of Melandra Crescent with their conspicuous display, which has been condemned as flashy and ostentatious.

Next-door neighbour Karen Ellis said: 'They were the first on the street to have two dogs destroyed, the first to have two kids inside, and now this. It's non-stop with them.

'She's always out there, smoking on the step, too la-di-da for a fag indoors, pint glass full of cigarette ends on the windowsill, thinking she's better than us, and it boils my piss.

'We're all on the same Universal Credit, love. Nobody's better than anyone else around here. But there she is with a 2007 Ford Ka up on bricks like Lady fucking Muck.'

She added: 'There used to be a family with two Sky dishes, but we hounded them out as paedos.'

Dawn Hurst said: 'They want to keep their fucking noses out. So what if we've got two garden washing machines? Doesn't mean we're too proud to let joyriders on the run from the bizzies hide in our shed.'

Are you a common person being blanked at a posh garden party, or a ghost?

Everyone looking through you? Your presence unacknowledged and your words seemingly unheard? Are you from the spirit realm or simply a faux pas? Find out here ...

Why are you here?

A. In 1694, a great wrong was done. After you were drowned as a witch, the injustice of your demise resonated through time and condemned you to haunt the waking world.

B. You were invited by a friend of a friend who, you now realise, only extended the invitation because you were inconveniently present and didn't mean a word of it. But you failed to pick up the signals and came anyway, in unbranded jeans.

Do you know anyone?

A. Through bloodlines you can recognise the descendants of those who collaborated in your untimely death, and through them you hope to exact revenge.

B. The friend you came with, who is avoiding you. And two catering staff have given you sympathetic glances, which has made you feel even worse.

Can anyone see you?

A. No, they just feel a coldness, a sense that something is not right ... the skin-crawling sensation that a spectre is nearby.

B. No, they just feel a coldness, a sense that something is not right ... the skin-crawling sensation that a commoner is nearby.

What happens when you speak?

A. Guests shiver, touched by a presence from beyond the grave.

B. Guests shudder, touched by a presence from a new-build estate.

Are you bored?

A. Extremely. For more than 300 years I've heard them bark on about how inheritance tax should be abolished and how this country would be a success if led by someone of breeding.

B. Thoroughly. All night they've barked on about the unfairness of inheritance tax and how we should bring Cameron back because he at least managed to marry a baroness.

When can you leave?

A. Only when my bones are buried in consecrated ground. Which won't be any time soon as they've sold off the bit of the estate with the churchyard in to Center Parcs.

B. Right now. Notice? Why would they notice?

How did you score?

Mostly As. You're dead and will never know peace until you get the attention of one of these ignorant nose-in-the-air bastards. Good luck with that.

Mostly Bs. You're lower class and will know peace the moment you're on your own, sinking a pint in a Harvester. And that ghost that was there can piss off as well.

Living near a Waitrose makes you a 12 per cent better person

A WAITROSE within a mile of your home improves your wisdom, altruism and lovemaking by 12 per cent.

Researchers found that residents within walking distance of the store gave more to charity, made charming dinner guests and were very good at playing at least two musical instruments.

Dr Martha Fletcher said: 'Every decision a Waitrose shopper makes is unfailingly correct. It's like the teaching of the Buddha, but cosier and less foreign.'

Waitrose shopper Torin Plunkett said: 'Paying more for groceries is an act of self-improvement. I don't want to be better than you, but I just am.'

The researchers also found that people who live near an Aldi have psychic powers that are often, but not always, used for evil.

Meanwhile, people who live near an Asda have an extra finger and are regularly attacked by crows.

Downwardly mobile millennial hoping for working-class son

A MAN who has given up hope of a comfortable upbringing for his children has refocused on giving them the credibility of being working class.

Richard Sweeney, aged 42, cannot afford the foreign holidays or multiple cars of his own childhood, and will instead reward the son he and his wife are expecting with a gritty, impoverished background that will pay dividends later.

He explained: 'There's nothing worse than feigning being middle class and being exposed as poor, so we're going the other way.

'We're preparing him for reduced circumstances. His crib will be a drawer, he'll have his own door key aged four, and there won't be any books or art in the house whatsoever.

'We can't afford private school and can't move into a better catchment, so he'll be at the condemned comprehensive down the road, leaving with pitiful GCSE grades and a mentality well-suited to shovelling shit or putting stuff on a conveyor belt.

'With any luck, he'll develop a penchant for cheap lager, going to the dogs on weekends and spitting at bus stops. You know, a happy and fulfilled life.'

Sweeney added: 'Me? I got a first from Cambridge and I'm a casting director. But there's not much money in it.'

University of Life brings in tuition fees

STUDENTS HOPING to move on to higher education from the University of Life must now pay a four-figure annual sum.

The UL's BSc in Street Savvy has a worldwide reputation for excellence, having produced successful graduates such as Lord Sugar and Jamie Oliver, while Cara Delevingne and Prince Harry both gained BAs in Being Born Beautiful and/ or Rich.

Such courses have traditionally been free, but from September students who opt to learn by getting their hands dirty will pay – whether with cash, payday loans or an addiction to crystal meth.

Defending the introduction of the £9,000 yearly fees, the government said: 'Is it really fair that hardworking British families have to pay for their kids' education at some uni that used to be a motorway service station, while benefit scroungers can get it gratis just by selling snide Armani jumpers their mate Shannon got off some geezer in Poplar?'

MP for Clacton Nigel Farage, himself a UL graduate, said: 'I studied free for my degree in Good Sound Common Sense. I'd very much like that opportunity for all British people, but unfortunately too many illegal immigrants are abusing the system.

'I can't give any specific examples of this, but as my old tutor always used to say, it stands to reason, doesn't it?'

Son of retired factory worker wishes people could tell

A MAN whose father worked in a factory his whole life wishes there were recognisable external signs of his gritty credentials.

Brand manager Joe Mead, aged 48, is not reticent in bringing up his dad's long service in manufacturing but wishes it was clear that he has struggled his way up to become the kind of wanker who does his big shop at M&S.

He said: 'If it were just subtly obvious, when I get out of my Audi, that I'm actually salt-of-the-earth, rough-hewn stock, I think it'd really come across well.

'Granted, factory jobs were decently paid then, so there was food on the table etcetera, but Dad came home in dirty overalls. Now that's an authenticity you simply can't buy.

'There's a real difference in the way people regard me when they find out he did ten-hour shifts bolting aircraft together. People realise that I became a twat in a bollocks job through hard graft, and that's the beauty of social mobility in this country.

'I'm racking my brains for a look to make my circumstances obvious. Dad wears a 40-year-old Buzzcocks T-shirt, but that's a him thing rather than some kind of class signifier. Besides, I'm not sure it would go with my expense account gut.

'Why can't it be like freckles or something? If I just gave off a vibe of unpretentious parentage I'd be served so much quicker in pubs.'

Oxbridge graduate or cocaine dealer:

who's really got their shit together?

We each walk our own path. Even within one family, one child may achieve a first from Oxford and the other may receive 18 months for possession with intent to supply. But which one is really winning at life?

Employment
Oxford graduate. Sends off 1,000 job applications in a year. Has three interviews, all found through contacts. Still not employed.

Cocaine dealer. Self-starting entrepreneur who doesn't wait for an employer to sort him out and is out on his bike actively looking for clients. Works all hours. An exemplar of the Thatcherite spirit, though he still claims benefits.

Finance
Oxford graduate. £45,600 in debt. Looking for a graduate entry-level role paying c. £25,000 p.a. Because degree is in English Literature, believes these numbers are workable.

Cocaine dealer. £100K in the bank and steady access to a product that is proven never to fall in demand. Besides, he saved plenty of money when he was inside, except child support payments.

Transferable skills
Oxford graduate. Studying things and answering questions on them, which appears not to be as desirable to the employment market as was made out.

Cocaine dealer. Accounting, relationship management, networking, price-setting, juggling credit, SEO, running social media, business Dutch and Albanian.

Philosophy
Oxford graduate. Read Marx and so understands that society is divided into a base and superstructure, with the relations of production constituting the economic structure of society.

Cocaine dealer. Can talk equal bollocks to the above after only two lines.

Reality
Oxford graduate. Has read Peter L. Berger and Thomas Luckmann's *The Social Construction of Reality*. Claims to understand it.

Cocaine dealer. Shanked a rival dealer in the prison showers and spent five days in isolation, completely naked. That's fucking reality, mate.

Love life
Oxford graduate. None. A book in the background of a profile picture is an immediate swipe left in this town.

Cocaine dealer. Wife, ex-wife, girlfriend, other girlfriend, ex-girlfriend, some romantic involvements with customers. Looks after all of them financially.

Piers Courtnay Gough-Calthorpe
Oxford graduate. Piers? I know Piers, rowed with him, pulled all-nighters in the library with him ... Great laugh, his dad owns half of Berkshire.

Cocaine dealer. Just made nine grand off Piers.

Social climber draws the line at opera

A CONSULTANT surgeon committed to scaling class barriers has refused to ever attend another fucking opera.

Dr James Janssen has been slowly progressing through England's hierarchy since primary school but, at the age of 54, has finally reached a point he will not ask his ears or his arse to endure.

He said: 'Joining the Freemasons was bad enough, but this? Three hours of bellowing and screeching in frigging German? Fuck that.

'Christ, they're clever, up there at the top of the pyramid. They didn't get there by accident. The obstacles in your way are many and varied. Just when you finally get the right wife, they blindside you with this.

'I've got the London townhouse, I've got the country pile, I'm a Garrick member and I held out for a CBE because I'm not a fucking lollipop lady. I accepted my invitation to Glyndebourne with grace and aplomb. But it was yet another test designed to weed out the plebs, and hats off, they succeeded. I'd rather be back in my Leeds terrace watching *Russ Abbot's Saturday Madhouse*, drinking cherryade than go through that again. In fact, that's the memory I retreated to.

'You win, aristocrats. You flushed me out. If enjoying Rossini is the price of admission, turn me away at the door. It reminded me of the NatWest pigs anyway.'

Sir Sholto Cook-Basford said: 'Yes, I did think that would do the trick.'

Striving family exchange TV too big for their living room for Aga too big for their kitchen

A FAMILY on the way up have exchanged a television far too large for their front room for an oven far too large for their kitchen.

Teresa Connolly's promotion meant she could finally afford a home big enough to accommodate the 98-inch Samsung QLED TV, but their move up in society meant they had to sell it and buy a 58-inch Aga Dual Control instead.

She explained: 'Back then, friends would come round to watch the *Love Island* final and we'd order in pizza. The contestants were life-sized across a whole wall, like a tapestry with fake tan.

'Now, our acquaintances and business associates are invited for dinner parties where we discuss prestige television while serving beef bourguignon slow-cooked in an Aga the size of an industrial cremator we have to squeeze past.

'It cost three times what the telly did and has to be left on all the time, even at night, again like the telly. It really heats up the kitchen to unbearable levels.

'We still have a television, but it can't be larger than 40 inches and has to be Bang & Olufsen. I thought the children would miss it but they're so busy with marimba lessons and racquet sports.

'Do I cook on the Aga? I don't really have time. I'm too busy working to afford a house big enough for the Aga. When I do, we'll buy a freestanding roll-top bath for a bedroom too small for it.'

Man celebrates pay rise by choosing slightly more expensive version of everything for the rest of his life

A MAN is celebrating a pay rise by buying slightly more costly versions of the same boring things, it has been confirmed.

Rod Barratt's new-found position as area sales manager will be reflected in changes to his lifestyle, including adding avocado to his burrito when presented with the option, putting the expensive petrol in his car for long journeys and buying pre-chopped carrots.

Barratt said: 'There's no way I'm wasting this on something like a once-in-a-lifetime holiday or a fancy car. That stuff's for mugs. I'm spreading it nice and thin.'

To celebrate, Barratt booked a meal at a slightly more expensive restaurant than he normally goes to and got a taxi both ways.

He added: 'We went out to dinner last and had the third-cheapest wine on the menu, instead of the second-cheapest. I guess that's just who I am now.

'I'll also be enjoying Netflix in 4K+ HDR, and I've added movies to my satellite package. This must be basically what Jeff Bezos lives like.'

You never got piano lessons as a child. Here's how to process your trauma

DID YOUR neglectful narcissistic parents refuse to fork out £38 a week so you could win success in adult life by performing *Für Elise* at half-speed? Work through it ...

Let it out

Even if you don't feel it, deep down there's a lot of repressed resentment about being musically stunted. You could have been the next Mozart if those bastards had granted your unvoiced wish to study the piano. Let yourself weep, sticking on some Rachmaninoff or Chopin and drinking heavily if it helps the tears to flow.

Surround yourself with artists

Your parents' selfishness may have stopped you ever becoming the world's greatest composer, or the next Tim Rice-Oxley from Keane, but you can still be a hanger-on. Become a freak who stands outside stage doors hoping to get your programme signed by Víkingur Ólafsson. Warm yourself in the piano-playing light you were lamentably denied.

Tell people about it, subtly

To truly heal emotionally, bring it up whenever someone mentions a piano, the illegal ivory trade or Billy Joel. Look wistfully away and say that you 'never had the opportunity' to play the piano, allowing others to infer the destitution and neglect of a childhood spent without even *Chopsticks*.

Try to recall their generosity in other areas

Did they once take you to Blackpool? Or buy you a bike? It can't possibly heal you - you'll still never recover your self-esteem and will lurch from one miserable, disastrous relationship to another. But while they will never be piano lessons, these small consolations where they at least tried will help you to be strong.

Have a go at your parents

The final step in the healing process is to absolutely let rip at those toxic abusers who pretend life is worth living without knowing how to play a C-minor scale. If they come back with excuses like, 'But we had a piano and you never touched it' or, 'You can have them now, if it means that much to you,' storm out of the house and never see them again.

Upwardly mobile man despised by those above, those below and his peers

A MAN striving to better himself and move beyond his modest origins is hated by the class above, the class below, his peers and his own family.

35-year-old Jack Browne, who went to Cambridge then Sandhurst and now works in the City, believed he would be a classic success story but has only made himself an object of ridicule and contempt to all.

Father Gary Browne said: 'I can't stand him. Coming around here all highfalutin reading his books, acting like an end terrace with a shared ginnel's beneath him.

'I'm gratified to find his neighbours in Kensington all look down on him and his workmates in the City call him Jack Ryanair because they discovered he flew on it to Magaluf once.

'Not that any of his mates will see him now. He can buy as many pints as he wants but by the very act of daring to dream of earning more and living somewhere else he's betrayed them and they all think he's a prick. You get what you deserve in this life, son.'

Professor Joseph Harbottle, a former tutor of Jack, said: 'It is pathetic when we encounter these people turning their back on their own. Who wouldn't hate him for quoting Foucault in a black polo-neck? Who among the educated cannot despise this dog on its hind legs?

'He's stolen opportunities the wealthy have rightfully paid for. He's put on airs; he's aping his betters without for a second understanding their quiet, inborn privilege. Shaking up a perfectly well-balanced class system just to feel good about himself. Egotistical prick.'

Browne said: 'I don't understand why everyone dislikes me so much. Perhaps I need to climb even higher.'

Working classes 'must express themselves only through National Theatre productions'

THE LOWER orders have been asked only to make their thoughts and feelings known in critically acclaimed theatre productions on London's South Bank.

Adam Peschanski, artistic director for the National Theatre, has requested that anyone from a low-income household, working manual jobs or residing in the north should express themselves solely through drama.

He said: 'Please, no novels. Stay out of film, and the contemporary arts are not for the likes of you.

'No, the medium for the impoverished – both financially and, even worse, spiritually – is the London stage. Specifically, our stage, once per season, in a damning but necessary exposé of your lives of total misery for entertainment.

'We'll cast actors who can enunciate, because your message is more powerful when it can be heard in the circle seats. It'll win Oliviers and make far more difference than shouting things at football matches, holding misspelled signs in the streets or voting Tory.'

Barnsley resident Sharon Hodder said: 'The council have said the only way to get the damp in my rented house sorted is to turn my life story into a cycle of six rehearsed readings performed by Jodie Comer.

'I'm more a fan of commedia dell'arte, but I'll string together some bollocks about having six kids by the time I was 13. That'll get a standing ovation and transfer to the West End for a limited run.'

Successful man urged always to remember shite childhood of poverty

A MAN who has achieved everything he ever wanted in life is constantly told he should never forget his difficult and unpleasant upbringing.

Neil Hodge, aged 49, who left school at 16 but went on to found several businesses and achieve a doctorate, would happily forget skipping dinners to save money and getting a new school blazer for Christmas, but people bring it up every day.

He said: 'My advice to my teenage self? Don't be successful, because you won't be able to enjoy it without some fucker dragging up the past.

'If it's not my mum saying, "Never forget your roots," even though I'd quite like to, as they were rubbish, it's some arsehole on a podcast making me relive my years on a sink estate so everyone can get off on it.

'You'd think I could just enjoy my flash cars and massive house, but apparently I have a duty to share my aspirational story. So off we go talking about how I used to cadge stale bread from an industrial bakery again.

'I holidayed in the Dutch Antilles last year. Anyone? No. The only holidays I had as a child were camping in a borrowed tent on a farmer's field? Now you're fucking interested.'

Bill Mackenzie, who went to school with Neil, said: 'I'd never want Neil to feel bad just because he had to borrow my trainers for PE because his mum couldn't buy him any. But I would like him to give me a hundred thousand pounds.'

Broken espresso machine temporarily demotes family down a social class

A FAMILY have temporarily dropped two rungs down the social ladder as they await repairs on their coffee machine.

The Adlers, of Houghton-le-Spring, made the devastating discovery that they were letting their whole street down when 52-year-old Mary attempted to make her morning espresso and received nothing but a mug of tepid grey backwash.

Even more bitter than the instant coffee they were forced to choke down was the realisation that failure of a kitchen appliance had dealt their already precarious position in the social hierarchy a real blow.

Mrs Adler said: 'I could swear nobody saw me buying the Douwe Egberts. But at the school gates, at 3.20pm that same day, everyone knew.

'Despite our steady dual income and our five-bedroom home, that Sage Bambino Plus was the only thing keeping our heads above the water. Until we get it fixed, we're in a very tricky position.

'It's not just the coffee. It's the special Italian barista quality of the coffee, like we were sipping it in a Sicilian side street. Now all we have to drink are kale smoothies and the purified water from our filter tap.

'The community has been very sympathetic, in a patronising way that makes it clear we're now their inferiors. Apparently there was talk of doing a colour run to raise funds to help but they couldn't trust us to spend the money wisely.

'Still, we've learned to appreciate what's real in life, like boiling a kettle. And it's given the children a gritty tale of misery to exploit in Oxford interviews.'

No progress on Essex prime minister

THE PEOPLE of Essex have admitted the dream of seeing one of their own leading the country from Downing Street is no closer.

While Britain has had three female prime ministers and one from an ethnic minority, and even though one of those four actually won an election, there has been no progress made on a leader from the Fake Tan County.

Civil servant Jacob Masters said: 'We have had several prime ministers from north London, just a short train ride away. But the gulf is seemingly unbridgeable.

'Despite the advances achieved by so many other of society's disadvantaged, and despite Westminster being relatively handy for a Westfield, there's a real dearth of candidates. In the last 50 years the closest we've had is Alex James.

'The vision of a bejewelled, tracksuited prime minister with megawatt veneers beaming out from a permatanned face, arm around Germany's chancellor calling him "mate", letting their pitbull shit on Whitehall and never bothering to pick it up – that's inspirational.

'But until Rylan or the GC join the Conservatives, we're stuck. Without an Argos-chain-wearing, stiletto-heeled hero to take the reins of power, telling Japan we're "well jel" of their productivity but they can leave import tariffs out innit, our county will go unrepresented.'

MP for Basildon and Billericay Katy West said: 'Being prime minister would be fucking wicked, though, innit.'

Eliza Doolittle a 'filthy class traitor'

HUMBLE COCKNEY flower-seller Eliza Doolittle is nothing more than a dirty traitor to the proletariat, it is alleged.

Socialist firebrand and Communist Party member Jack Turpin says that the iconic heroine of *My Fair Lady* has kowtowed to the whims of the petit bourgeoisie and undermined the struggle.

He said: 'From the moment she started singing "Wouldn't It Be Loverly?", I knew she hadn't the right consciousness. Would you really prefer chocolate to eat and a warm fire than the elimination of the parasite landlord class?

'Abandoning her roots to become another simpering upper-middle-class woman who extracts wealth from the labours of others is as despicable as it gets. And the rain in Spain falls mainly on mountainous regions. I'm doing Geography A Level.'

Noah Tabakin, Turpin's English Literature teacher, said: 'As I've told Jack, Ms Doolittle is a fictional character created by a renowned socialist. It's a pleasant story about a woman discovering her independence.'

Turpin retorted: 'It runs in complete contravention to Marxist principles. Under Mao, Eliza would be sent to a re-education camp and be all the better for it.

'Unless, of course, she's a spy. That would be fine, actually. I could enjoy the musical if she was going to use her information to have Henry Higgins executed after the revolution.'

Aspirational woman orders first set of beef cheeks

A WOMAN has set in place plans to move up a social class by eating progressively more obscure cuts of meat.

Imogen Shaw of Chorlton began by upgrading her usual steak to a different, apparently better slab of cow, and plans to branch out into weird bits of fish and birds shortly.

She said: 'I need people who don't know me well to believe I'm richer and more sophisticated than I am for reasons I don't fully understand. In other words, I'm English.

'I soon realised an easy way to do this was to order expensive cuts of meat and act like I knew why this mattered. Also you have to eat them near-raw.

'It has been a learning curve, pretending you prefer blobby eggs of fish that look like some sort of slime-based children's toy instead of a battered cod from down the chippy, but nobody said social climbing was easy.

'Some of it does appear to result from a kind of sick animal torture porn - for example, foie gras - but we're not yet at the point where they do it next to the table, so fine. I even crack lobsters, because apparently seafood is fancier if you're doing half the work yourself.

'It's all worth it to seem classy. Soon I'll be recommending delicacies to people that sound like they were generated by a masochistic AI. Enjoy your sun-dried pheasant toe and twisted pork nipples.

'Plus, in the end, it is easier than having to learn about wine.'

This week in Mash History: steerage passengers on *Titanic* struggle to surmount class barriers, 1912

ONE OF the most horrifying, preventable tragedies of recent history, James Cameron's *Titanic* is based on a ship of the same name that sank in the North Atlantic.

But while today we think of the ship as an egalitarian utopia where the Irish jigged and romance bloomed regardless of status, recent evidence suggests not all passengers were able to overcome their inbuilt sense of place.

While ticket classes were based on class preferences, with steerage passengers sensibly denied access to the Turkish baths, à la carte restaurant and grand staircase which would only confuse them, third-class passengers also hit a class ceiling when it came to safe evacuation in the event of disaster.

A recently uncovered eyewitness report said: 'No more than a single collision with an iceberg and without warning the lower decks seem to have lost all sense of pride in themselves.

'On the voyage previous, these same men were steadfast in their identities. They recognised they had neither the breeding nor the commitment to earn a first-class ticket and accepted it. Now? They clamour to be allowed on the upper decks.

'What makes a man so dismissive of entry to our smoking room one day, yet so desperate for admittance to our lifeboat the next? Surely, they should be hardy enough to endure the Atlantic unfettered by boats?

'I have also witnessed a heretofore unknown phenomenon: a lady adamantly refusing to let passengers board our half-full lifeboat, aggressively referring to technicalities and threatening to speak with the captain. I did not catch her surname but believe she went by "Karen".'

And so the lower-class passengers were unable to overcome their assigned stations, or get past large metal gates, and suffered the unfortunate but fair consequences of hypothermia and drowning.

Next week: to 1979, when Margaret Thatcher proved that with hard work and bold thinking you can be evil no matter your socio-economic origins.

Meritocracy no use if you're thick, complain cretins

ORDINARY MORONS from across Britain have complained a meritocracy is no use to those without drive, talent or basic intelligence.

While previous generations could always blame their failures on the oppression and lack of opportunities inherent in the class system, social mobility has left the thick and downtrodden with nobody but themselves to blame.

Halfwit proletarian Sarah Palmer said: 'Say what you like about my grandfather going down the mines at 14, or my great-grandmother getting knocked up by the master of the house then fired, there was proper subjugation then.

'Not like now, when everybody's meant to be able to achieve. Ignoring that a lot of us are genuinely, unassailably dense so it presents no benefit at all. Hurtful if anything.

'Back in the old days, we used to tell a cosy tale of an uncle who was an accounting genius but got kicked out of his job for the bank manager's son. All horseshit, but it warmed the cockles of our simple hearts to know our penury and hardship were in no way our responsibility.

'It was better when the rich was properly evil, in monocles and striking beggars with their canes. Bring back them bastards, I say.'

Sociologist Dr Louise Blundell said: 'Britain isn't a meritocracy, but if we falsely claim you can scale the class structure through hard work and dedication, everyone blames themselves for their own lack of advancement. And that really keeps them in their place.'

Friend with wife, children and six-figure job thinks he's better than you

A FRIEND who has a stable marriage, two happy children, a fulfilling, high-earning career, a big house and an expensive car believes it makes him superior to you.

Mark Reynolds, who has known you since school, gave away that he considers himself to have made more of his life than you have when he not only bought all the drinks but offered to 'help you out' with a taxi home.

Old pal Jake Dobson said: 'We've got different priorities, that's all.

'I wouldn't want all the sellout wife and kids stuff, which is why I never stay in a relationship longer than a year, and he wouldn't want my - the things I - what I've got.

'Sure, if you judge by material success, or stability, or I suppose long-term happiness, then he's doing better. But he knows I don't walk that path. Doesn't mean he's got any right to set himself above me.

'He was going on about this amazing California holiday he'd had with the family, a bit insensitive when he knows I spent the summer on remand and it wasn't even my fault.

'I bit back the urge to say, "And that makes you better than me, does it?"'

Reynolds said: 'I think he's back living at his dad's again, aged 38. I mean, I've only got so much pity to give.'

Hummus is our equivalent of Shippam's Beef Paste, says Lebanese labourer

What to do when offered loaves by a bread-making neighbour

Waitrose top for organic vegetables, customer service and MILFs

Montessori school teaches children how to charge money for bullshit

Bookies, key-cutters and Cash Converters: six establishments where the middle classes fear for their very lives

Grandparents demand ridiculous original nicknames

Middle class the real unskilled labour

Nine phrases your nice teenager wasn't brought up to say

Missing woman found under throw pillow avalanche

Middle-class woman mortified about how much brie she ate last night

Self-loathing as an Art Form:

How to be
middle class

THE WORKING classes hate the middle classes, obviously, for putting on airs and pretending their children are clever for having wooden toys. And the upper classes despise the middle classes, rightly, for their pathetic pretence that manners are more important than enormous wealth. But neither of them hates the middle classes with the towering, fiery loathing of the middle classes. They spend every minute of every day loathing their peers, their friends, their family and that arsehole in the mirror with his ironic T-shirts and his piss-easy homeworking job. God, he's such an unbearable knobhead. Dip into the following orgy of enmity and remember: every ounce of the nauseating abhorrence you feel is entirely justified. These people really are the worst scum.

Hummus is our equivalent of Shippam's Beef Paste, says Lebanese labourer

A LEBANESE labourer has explained to Britain once again that hummus is not considered at all fancy in its country of origin.

Omar Haddad, who works as a bricklayer, has hummus for his lunch every day because it is considered a cheap, basic foodstuff anyone with an office job would sneer at.

He said: 'Britain, get over it. They're chickpeas. They're just about the cheapest known foodstuff and one step above what we give to pigs.

'Round here, the peasantry's been eating hummus for at least 700 years. Me and the lads on the site get through a few kilos of the stuff every day, delivered in big industrial tubs.

'Yet you bang on about it like it's Beluga caviar. How deprived is the UK that you think legume mash is an exotic food that makes the consumer special?

'And you pay £2.50 a pot for the factory-made crap in M&S. What happened? Can you not mix chickpeas, sesame, garlic and oil? Is that too complicated? Didn't you used to have an empire?

'I know you lot struggle with anything foreign, so let's put it in a way you'll understand. Hummus is like Shippam's Beef Paste: common, cheap and your grandad likes it because he doesn't have to chew.'

What to do when offered loaves by a bread-making neighbour

BREAD IS cheaply available from shops, yet your smug neighbour has once again brought around one of his hot artisanal loaves. These are your options:

Accept graciously

The polite thing to do condemns you to a life as a baker's guinea pig, constantly fed new sourdough, required to give feedback on a gritty brown rye loaf day and night, never being for one moment negative to protect the bread-maker's delicate feelings, even though his work looks and tastes like a house brick. Never do this.

Refuse point-blank

So offensive you could live here for a further 30 years and never speak to your neighbour again. But worth it not to spend three decades presented with regular floury dowries. To really rub pink Himalayan salt in his dough, mention what a coincidence it is him appearing with a loaf just as you're popping out for Hovis.

Claim medical issues

Accept the loaf but explain you can't eat it. But - crucially - don't blame it on gluten. These people are wise to the ways of the coeliac. If the loaf isn't already gluten-free, they'll be round with a second in no time. Instead, claim an intolerance for salt, sugar, flour, water and yeast. Offer to take the loaf anyway as you're passing the duck pond later.

Accept but give mindful feedback

In offering bread, your neighbour isn't providing sustenance but insisting you feed his ego. Calling his cob 'one big, fat fucking doughy air bubble' or remarking that his baguettes were so crusty they lacerated your gums will deflate that ego smartly.

Offer passive disrespect

Accept the healthy kalamata olive loaf, saying it will be perfect for a bacon butty. Your neighbour will assume you're joking and meant a prosciutto open sandwich until you knock on his door ten minutes later, offering him a docker's wedge dripping in budget-brand ketchup. Traumatised at the violence done to his offering, he will not bake for you again.

Dispose of immediately

Thank your neighbour effusively for your loaf and, while he stands there, take it and reverently place it in your food waste bin, murmuring, 'To the precious Buddha, I make this offering.' Close the lid, say 'Life to life' with a pious expression and watch him take his confused leave. You won't get round-robin letters from him at Christmas. Ah well.

Waitrose top for organic vegetables, customer service and MILFs

WAITROSE IS the best supermarket for fresh produce and highly attractive middle-aged women, research has found.

A study found that a Waitrose branch can increase local house prices by 50 per cent, while customers praised the store's tasty organic fare, knowledgeable staff and the way it is teeming with smoking hot, sexually confident mums.

56-year-old Peter Reddy said: 'I think the deli counter is excellent, the black pudding-coated Scotch eggs are truly of artisan quality and the scallops are to die for. Also, it is the most mental boner fest.

'Waitrose is like the local MILF HQ, or "Moonbase MILF", as I call it.

'Seriously, I don't mean to sound like a perv, but I had to repeatedly smash my raging groin into a chiller cabinet just so I could go and pay.'

Mother-of-two Lorna Nash said: 'I'm straight but I come here mainly for the MILFs. Compared to other supermarkets, Waitrose MILFs are delicious. They could be actresses in daytime soaps. The minute I walk in the door I'm bisexual.'

She added: 'That's why it's the best supermarket, even though it's nine fucking quid for a fish pie.'

Montessori school teaches children how to charge money for bullshit

THE SKILL of conning the wealthy to pay a fortune for fuck all is the most important lesson Montessori schools can teach, their heads have confirmed.

The unorthodox institutions have weathered criticisms like, 'It costs £30,000 a year for my seven-year-old to play with twigs?' and shown thousands of privileged children that a business model of raking in cash for bollocks is a pathway for life.

Headteacher Catherine Johnson said: 'I missed out on so much as a child. I learned economics at private school and believed you needed a genuine product or service to make money.

'Here, we let children explore for themselves. They get hours of first-hand experience bashing magnets together while being silently watched by a teacher with no formal qualifications, knowing that their parents are paying thousands of pounds for the privilege.

'That leads them to an understanding you can't get from books. They learn the Emperor's New Clothes business model from the inside-out in a hands-on way.

'Using these practical techniques, our alumni go on to make more and more money from flimsier and flimsier bullshit. They may miss out on essential skills like literacy and numeracy, but you can pay other people to do that if you can sell a gut health smoothie for £36 a bottle.

'And often these children, rich as they are, are stunningly dull. This gives them anecdotes about Montessori education they can fill the silences in their marriages with.'

Bookies, key-cutters and Cash Converters: six establishments where the middle classes fear for their very lives

ON THE mean high streets of Britain there are retailers where the comfortable fear to tread. These are the providers of specialist services that get their urban grit in your eye ...

Bookmakers

Ducking through the proper punters' vape clouds, your testicles retract as you belatedly realise you have no clue how to place a bet. The dead-eyed stare of the girl taking your fiver while benefits claimants lose £20 a spin on casino machines ensures that next time you want to make football 'more interesting', you'll do it from your phone.

Key-cutters

As a *Guardian* reader, you greatly admire the work Timpson does with ex-offenders. In practice, the two lads behind the counter fall silent as you enter and you feel like fresh meat on C-wing. They're helpful, but you're too engrossed in their homemade tattoos to absorb why you need a heavy-duty fob on your replacement car key.

Cash Converters

Replacing your teenager's lost phone with a pre-loved one is good for the planet and your pocket, but that warm green glow fades fast as you wait behind an emphysemic pensioner haggling to get an extra £3.20 for all their worldly goods. Is that iPhone legit, or stolen by an addict? Wait, you recognise that case. That's his lost phone.

Backstreet garage

The mechanic favours you with a nod but no actual words as you try to describe the intermittent squeak on the passenger side. You feel like you're in a troll's cave but you might come back, because the official Vauxhall dealer never calls a repair 40 quid for cash because it's Friday and he wants tax-free beer money.

City pub

How rough can a pub just off a main shopping street be? Extremely. Nobody speaks, a humorously aggressive sign discourages payment by card, and the barmaid helpfully puts 80p of your change in the tip jar without asking. Your group sets a new record for downing pints as none of you dares say another word.

Freezer centre

Everyone in here knows you're slumming. They hiss under their breath as you block their way. What are you looking for, Wagyu steaks? Langoustines? Piss off. All you achieve is helping an elderly lady too wizened to reach the depths of the freezer for Findus Crispy Pancakes. And she resented you for it.

Grandparents demand ridiculous original nicknames

A PAIR of middle-class grandparents have confirmed that names like Granny and Grandad are too boring for people as unique and special as them.

Saskia Belton and her husband Henry have told their family they are thrilled to be grandparents but will not be answering to any traditional titles such as Gran, Nan or Grampy.

Saskia said: 'As a trendy, dynamic older woman I don't want to be trailed by a child shouting something frumpy when all my other friends are being called interesting things like Whizzy and Gangnam.

'I would consider something that is popular abroad, like Abuela or Nonna, but I don't really want people to think my daughter did it with a foreigner.

'I'm also interested in something that makes absolutely no sense but sounds cool, like Fancy or Peach.

'And as for Henry, I haven't felt a twinge of attraction towards him since 1987, so having to call him Grandpa would just add insult to injury. Maybe if he was renamed Bubba or Big Poppa, it would get my juices flowing a bit.'

Middle class the real unskilled labour

WHITE-COLLAR, MIDDLE-CLASS professionals earning in the high five figures are the real unskilled labour in Britain, experts have confirmed.

While statisticians continue to refer to those who provide vital services as 'unskilled', those with job titles like 'Digital Business and Product Journey Manager' and 'Relationship Officer' have escaped scrutiny.

Professor Toby Palfreyman of the Institute for Studies said: 'Sending an email isn't a skill. You've clicked a mouse, dickhead. Well done. No wonder your father isn't proud.

'The only challenge in these jobs is maintaining a straight face as you say you're "implementing key competencies". Compare a "skillset" in "organic search", "agile methodologies" and "cascade communication" with the unskilled, without who there would be no cleaners, carers or food in shops.

'If you're asked what your labour actually produces and you reply, "You mean the key deliverables?", then you being kicked to death outside JD Sports would be a net gain for society.'

Forklift driver Carl Broomfield said: 'At the end of the day, bullshit jobs keep them out of trouble. It's like a youth club for people with humanities degrees from Russell Group universities.

'I often say that the prevalence of those spongers disproves Keynes's theory that automation would lead to a 15-hour workweek, but rather has led to a pernicious form of wage slavery whereby the subject is unable to see the fundamental nihilism at the heart of their existence so can't attain the consciousness necessary to cast off the subjugation represented by contemporary managerial feudalism.

'And the lads down the Red Lion agree.'

Nine phrases your nice teenager wasn't brought up to say

YOUR TEENAGER is not like the ape-like creatures hooting at bus stops. Your teenager is nice and well-mannered but unaccountably uses these uncouth phrases:

'It's my truth'

There's only one truth, surely? Nobody gets their own except Donald Trump, and he insists really hard. But apparently every Gen Z child has their own version of the truth that must be respected, even if it's bollocks from a knobhead on TikTok. Also, frequently 'his truth' does not match up with 'his internet history'.

'Wait, what?'

A moronic American non sequitur absorbed through sitcoms and used to convey confused bafflement at the simplest of statements, such as 'Bring the plates down from your bloody room.' Apparently, everything from going to bed to brushing teeth is now an utter surprise to them. And you just have to take it.

'I need to search it up'

Your teenager proclaims with confidence that she needs to 'search it up' while you repeat helplessly, 'It's *search for*, or *look it up!*' She's not listening. She's reading a recap of a show she's never watched because she's listening to a podcast about it later.

'She's angry at me'

It's angry with, not angry at, but you can't win this war

unless you ban everything with American dialect, which would mean no TV, no phone and no internet. And you and your spouse are halfway through *Modern Family* so that's not happening.

'I'm going gym'

The most bloodcurdling statement to come from your teenager's mouth. While they are at least exercising, you are forced to detain them, their gym bag and their grudging sneer to advise them about the fundamentals of English grammar. They may not thank you for this. Afterwards, consider taking up recreational alcoholism.

'No offence, but ...'

The standard precursor to any statement that will definitely offend you because it was designed to do so.

'It's more better than'

Slow your breathing, centre yourself and explain that better is already the comparative form of 'good', which means 'more' is superfluous. See also 'the most best'. Your restrained explanation will be met with a stare of aggressive incomprehension.

'For time'

As in 'But we won't get there for time, bro!' Try to resist driving directly into the base of a bridge.

'It's literally'

It is definitely not literally. If you point this out, you are literally wasting your breath. Instead, reassure yourself that ChatGPT is writing their homework anyway, so your dumbass kids will be fine.

Missing woman found under throw pillow avalanche

A WOMAN reported missing by her family has been found buried under an avalanche of throw pillows in her own home.

Tara Miller, who is currently recovering in hospital, admitted causing the pillow-slide after trying to fit on six new ones she had bought that day from Next.

She said: 'The settee, which nobody's allowed to sit on because it disturbs the arrangement, already had more than 168 throw and scatter pillows on it. In retrospect that was a few too many.

'I put the new ones on in descending size order according to custom, stepped back to admire it and heard an ominous creaking.

'The next thing I knew, I was buried in an avalanche of plushness, sequins, faux fur and curlicued script saying something about love. I tried to call out, but my voice was simply too muffled.'

Rescuers have been criticised for not searching beneath the pillows earlier even though the house's garden contained an ornate birdbath and the downstairs loo had four different Yankee Candles – both clues pointing to a bourgeois disaster.

Miller managed to survive for three days on a half-bottle of rosé and a packet of wasabi peas. The incident came a week after a Cotswolds man was rescued from within his own North Face clothing, having been trapped for over a week.

Middle-class woman mortified about how much brie she ate last night

AN EMBARRASSED mother-of-two is anxiously replaying the brie-fuelled conversations about house prices and grammar schools she had at a dinner party last night.

Judith Norris, aged 39, admitted that after the tamarind-marinated bavette steak the rest of the evening was a blur.

She continued: 'I could feel myself losing control early on with the stilton puffs. A couple of heads turned when I was waxing lyrical about the novels of Elena Ferrante.

'But by the time the cheeseboard came out, I was completely off the rails. Hot yoga, Tom Hardy, the perils of buy-to-let … I didn't give a shit. All I wanted was more brie.

'I'm pretty sure I had half the wheel, and I must have had gluten because I'm horribly bloated. Simon wasn't much better. I'm sure I remember him claiming he was going to found a free school.

'Was I cramming it in without even taking the rind off? I need help.'

Host Rachel Innes said: 'We were all pretty high on our own status. After they'd gone I binged six episodes of *The Crown*.'

Who says you can't transcend your origins? This radical Marxist revolutionary was privately educated

Working long hours for shit wages doesn't make you working class

Restaurant couple clearly on a voucher

An absolute bastard to heat: why you'd hate to live in a stately home

Cheeky street urchin just stole your identity

How to unnerve your oh-so-fucking-fancy new neighbours in five easy steps

Burberry, Kappa and other designer brands British chavs have enjoyed ruining

Couple's wedding theme is 'Look how rich our parents are'

The more essential your work the less you get paid, them's the rules, says capitalism

Student with £250K in trust fund asks to be paid back for half a Twix

You can get pregnant if you share a lane in the swimming pool: myths about comprehensives that grammar school kids believed

Are you a posh person getting pissed?

Six people you believe yourself superior to who earn three times your income

Rough family throws Gü ramekin away like it's rubbish

Woman claims to be both posh and Welsh

Nando's to add viewing gallery

Low life expectancy versus having to watch *Fleabag*: which is better?

Local hard family plans day of low-level troublemaking

Working dog adopted by non-working family

Jesus: toff or chav?

Know Your Enemy for the Class War:

The twats above

and

the scum below

IT'S ALL those other bastards that are the problem. Your particular point on the class spectrum is the perfect place to be: not dog-rough but not arsey. If everyone was like you, this country wouldn't be so bitterly divided. Unfortunately, the dog-rough below will insist on driving vans and having all-inclusive holidays in the Algarve, while those snooty wankers above continue to swan around with an air of marked superiority even though it's been repeatedly explained they're wrong by the films of Ken Loach. These are the ways and habits of your class enemies. Study them. Learn their vulnerabilities. Be ready to strike.

Who says you can't transcend your origins? This radical Marxist revolutionary was privately educated

THINK YOU'RE stuck with the prejudices and beliefs of the class you were born into? Guess again, as firebrand Marxist revolutionary Alfie Jillings's background proves.

Yes, despite spending his every waking moment fighting (online) for the proletariat, Alfie was actually a boarder at one of the better public schools! Take that, idiots who believe your privilege decides your politics!

And unbelievably, Alfie is calling for the dismantling of our capitalist system even though his own father is a board member of several City financial firms and a landlord! Seems not everything's inherited!

Alfie, who wants to violently overthrow the state and execute the rentier class, admits he was inspired by others who overcame their origins to spend their lives selflessly fighting for others, like his hero Jeremy Corbyn.

'You'd never guess it,' says Alfie, 'but Corbyn himself was raised in a 17th-century farmhouse and educated at a private prep and an exclusive grammar. Nonetheless, it didn't stop him spending his life battling for the working man.'

Too right, Alf, and he's far from the only one! Pol Pot was educated in Paris, Lenin's father was a hereditary nobleman and Fidel Castro went to private school! Only Stalin lets the side down by coming from poverty - and look how wrong he got it! So next time you condemn the privately educated as out-of-touch idiots ignorant of real Britons' concerns, stop! Alfie has Latin A Level, and he knows what's best for you even better than you do!

Working long hours for shit wages doesn't make you working class

BRITONS HAVE been informed that mere labouring for long hours in precarious jobs for minimum wage does not entitle them to call themselves working class.

Experts have explained to young people, people of colour, women, foreigners and southerners that just because their jobs could not be worse nor their wages lower does not mean they can use the hallowed epithet of 'working class' to describe themselves.

Francis Napper, author of *Old, White and Living in Barnsley: The English Working Class*, said: 'The very fact that these people are working at all makes them suspect. The truly authentic working classes are for the most part retired.

'When we say "working class" we mean salt-of-the-earth types who trod the cobbled streets of the 1950s to work in factories and are too busy scrubbing themselves in tin baths to think about identity politics and feminism.

'Some of these people claiming to be working class have fancy jobs like barista, sandwich artist and care worker. Well, you don't come home with a dirty face from those.

'The real working classes, from mines, steel mills or Sunderland, have earned their right to be reactionary, Brexit-voting Nigel Farage devotees. These others are nothing but arrivistes.'

22-year-old delivery driver Cody Hinkley said: 'I hoped I might be working class, because they count. But I ate an avocado once so I'm urban metropolitan elite.'

An absolute bastard to heat: why you'd hate to live in a stately home

EVER DREAMED of owning an 18-bedroom Georgian mansion in its own grounds? This is why you'd soon be running back to your flat above a Croydon kebab shop ...

Heating costs

You're already financially broken by energy bills. Now try heating four parlours, six galleries and a suite of guest rooms, with radiators installed in the 1930s and insulation from the 1830s. You sit in your armchair by a roaring fire, staring up at the vaulted ceilings where every therm of your money goes.

Maintenance

600 yards of banisters to polish, acres of carpet to hoover and the curtains are mouldy. Can you be arsed? Even if rich, you'll be employing more staff than Burton-on-Trent Travelodge. And at least one room will have a flimsy 17th-century carpet that can only be gently scoured with a thimble on a full moon or it'll disintegrate instantly.

Off the grid

Being miles from your neighbours sounds great, but living away from actual amenities such as mains sewerage is less romantic. You'll learn to be frugal with bog roll and to keenly anticipate the emptying of the septic tank. And, as you're two miles from a mobile mast and six miles from fibre, your internet access is fucked.

Doing 10,000 steps without leaving the house

Nipping into the next room to pop the kettle on is for scum in rabbit hutches. You trek across three different wings just to get a mobile charger and sprint to the dining room to reach your dinner before it goes cold. Sadly, without success. Lost your glasses? They could be in any one of 31,000 locations.

Something's always falling down

Like a city centre Wetherspoons, country houses only look nice on the outside. Every other week you'll have gleeful contractors explain that you have an extreme case of mimblerot or deathworm that will cost all your money to fix, and you can't ignore them because it's Grade II listed and English Heritage will drag your arse to court.

Ghosts

Houses that old are haunted by default. Every creak, groan and bang - and, because it's falling down, there are plenty - is a nobleman's murdered wife, or mistress, or maid. You'll go past three headless horsemen just to pour yourself another gin, and they're all behind you when you watch telly because they'd rather have *Newsnight* on.

Restaurant couple clearly on a voucher

A COMMON-LOOKING couple in a fancy restaurant were only there because of an internet voucher, according to fellow diners.

The overdressed pair were disconcertingly excitable because of underlying nervousness, stated regular patrons of Rovelli's in Bloomsbury.

Cassia Morris, a corporate consultant, said: 'Everything about them screamed "50 per cent off".

'They were talking in broad estuary accents then switching to ridiculous pseudo-posh tones when the waiter came to take their order.

'My suspicions were confirmed when they cut the bread rolls with butter knives.'

Solicitor Aloysius Draper said: 'If it wasn't for certain websites offering a two-for-one deal on the Wagyu porterhouse, I would never have to look at people like that except when they are fixing my boiler or driving me in a taxi.

'Our entire societal infrastructure is under threat from coupons.'

Restaurant manager Pippa Benn said: 'We're keen to encourage new customers to Rovelli's because nothing says "Welcome" like the thinly veiled hostility of people who have paid full price for a steak.'

After the couple left a tip based on the cost of their voucher, rather than the non-discounted bill, Benn added that they were subhuman scum who should be chased into the sea.

How to unnerve your oh-so-fucking-fancy new neighbours in five easy steps

THOSE WANKERS who moved in next door look like gentrifiers. Give them an inch and they'll replace the vape shop with a cupcake bakery. These tips should shut them up:

Have a clear-out

Or a 'declutter', as those up-themselves twats call it. Ideal items to declutter are disused fridges, stained mattresses or the broken remnants of fitted kitchens. Declutter them all the way to the garden and leave them there. They're the council's problem now. You've got *Homes Under the Hammer* to watch.

Get a dog

Only natural when they've got a cat. Make it a big dog, one that's naturally playfully aggressive and highly territorial. Reassure everyone it's safe by walking it on a massive chain. Calmly shout, 'He's just messing!' while it slavers and growls at your neighbours as they hurry into their car.

Put a sofa in the garden

Not weatherproof garden seating, but a proper fabric sofa made for a front room. Placement is very important. Too near the kerb and it looks like it's out for the bins. Instead, put it squarely on your patch of astroturf, facing the street, so you can enjoy a spliff and eight or so cans al fresco every evening. That'll show them and their fucking hornbeam hedge.

Build that illegal extension

On the cheap at mates' rates, meaning work continues

erratically on evenings and weekends for months. Ignore boring shit about planning permission or party wall agreements and finish with bare, functional breeze blocks. When hesitantly questioned about its purpose, explain that 19-year-old Nathan needs somewhere to party with his mates.

Become an entrepreneur

Finally, place an eye-catching sign outside your house proclaiming 'Hand Car Wash' or 'Nadines's Eyelash Extensions'. Run the business 24 hours and dare those pricks next door to dob you in to the benefits. And if they do, just hide the sign behind the sofa and carry on dealing.

Cheeky street urchin just stole your identity

A DIRTY-FACED barefoot rascal has stolen all your personal data and will use it to commit identity fraud.

Roguish nine-year-old James Bates, wearing a top hat with a busted crown and a purloined chrysanthemum in its band, deftly pickpocketed all your logins and passwords and is already using your account to buy bitcoin on the dark web.

He said: 'Cheers for your help, mister! What kind of a gent don't use a VPN in a Caffè Nero? You're begging to get taken and I ain't no type to turn a beggar down!

'Thanks to your generosity, sir, my fellow lads of the streets and I will be able to eat tonight, oh yes. You'll be seeing the Deliveroo debits presently! No more disgusting shoplifted Prime energy drinks for us. I'm so happy I could sing!

'Oh, come on, toff, don't get all angry and email the *Guardian*'s Consumer Champions. I'm merely the product of a broken society. Me ma and da ain't dead or nothing, but they work long hours and I'm forced to amuse myself with cybercrime. Have a heart.

'You'll get it all back from the banks so it's a victimless crime and leaves society all the richer. It's all in fun, fella! I'm impertinent and scrumping Apple products!'

The urchin added: 'Fuck, you're how overdrawn? This was a wasted effort. I should charge you.'

Couple's wedding theme is 'Look how rich our parents are'

AN ENGAGED couple have decided to theme their upcoming wedding around their parents' vast wealth.

Nancy Fitzherbert and Sebastian Kitt toyed with several motifs, including their shared love of snowboarding and Dubai breaks, before settling on a celebration of their family finances.

Fitzherbert said: 'Well, they are spending more than £130,000 on the day, so it just seemed an honest one that everyone could have fun with.

'The invitations are embossed with images of our family homes, we've ordered a cake shaped like Seb's dad's yacht and my dad's speech will dwell on wonderful moments we've had in luxury destinations around the world.

'There's a free bar with trained mixologists, continuing the theme of abundant money, and all the wedding cars will be borrowed from our next-door neighbour in Buckinghamshire. Who's Jamiroquai.'

The pair added that, in keeping with their theme, they will eschew the fashionable sentiment that their guests' presence is enough.

Fitzherbert said: 'Fuck that. The wedding list starts at £500.'

Burberry, Kappa and other designer brands British chavs have enjoyed ruining

CREATED A fashion brand synonymous with luxury? Pray that British football fans and estate kids don't take a liking to it and ruin it forever, like these:

Burberry

Once associated with class, style and sophistication – Audrey Hepburn wore a Burberry coat in the final scene of *Breakfast at Tiffany's* – until the late '90s, when hardcore hooligans decided their nova check hats paired beautifully with violence. Danniella Westbrook's head-to-toe embrace of the brand followed and rendered the check so toxic it's only just back on shelves two decades later.

Kappa

Anyone who attended comprehensive school during the heyday of this Italian sportswear brand is familiar with the insulting, belittling and entirely fair label 'Kappa slapper'. Those negative associations went mainstream with *Little Britain*'s Vicky Pollard and the Kappa logo is now the international symbol for teenage pregnancy.

Stone Island

The casual subculture has seen football crews fuck up brands like they fuck up provincial town centres on awaydays, but the one most thoroughly destroyed is Stone Island. To the extent that bars ban the clothing because the presence of that buttoned-on compass logo increases the chances of a patron being glassed. Also, Noel Gallagher wears it.

The North Face

Once beloved of sensible mums on the school run and rangy men obsessed with bagging Munros, which is far less sexual than it sounds, the jackets have been enthusiastically adopted by kids riding e-bikes on the pavement to steal your phone. Usually worn with grey trackies and Nike Air Max 95s, these coats will never see a mountain's summit. Pity them.

Adidas 3 Stripes

This sportswear staple was co-opted by proto-chavs back in the 1980s and has been anathema to the rest of society ever since. Briefly worn by Damon Albarn when he was cosplaying as working class, it's still best seen worn as a full tracksuit by a 14-year-old who stopped attending school at 12 with the full encouragement of his parents because they need his county lines money.

Balenciaga

Thrillingly expensive and abominably ugly, Balenciaga retains a following among the wealthy for now. However, it's developing a strong following among the bump-of-coke-off-a-car-key set and looks ready to be brought crashing down to the potholed tarmac early in 2025. The rough kids are wearing knock-offs, of course. They're too savvy to pay real money for this horrible shit.

Student with £250K in trust fund asks to be paid back for half a Twix

A 19-YEAR-OLD who drives a brand-new Prius and could not believe the student kitchen only had two ovens is at your door, asking for the 38p you owe her.

Although Rosie Calton receives an annual stipend greater than your parents' combined income, she strongly resents not receiving full payment from when she split an item of confectionery with you last week.

She continued: 'People take advantage. Just because I'm well-off doesn't mean I don't deserve to be fairly recompensed for a piece of gum, or the loan of a pen.

'Yes, it's small change, but it's the principle of the thing. Today it's a free Twix, tomorrow you want a lift, by the end of the week I'm basically an unpaid servant. And my proper trust fund, the one from my grandparents, doesn't kick in until I'm 21.

'I can be generous. I brought that bottle of champagne to your birthday even though we're not close, and I don't charge anyone for using my spare Bluetooth speaker in the shared kitchen.

'Anyway, do you have the money? Only I have to have it now because I'm going to the Cotswolds for the weekend, so I'll need it.'

Housemate Ryan said: 'Rosie is the stingiest bitch alive. She seems to think that everything in the bathroom comes free with rent. Thankfully, she'll be gone next year as she's doing an internship at the Treasury.'

The more essential your work the less you get paid, them's the rules, says capitalism

CAPITALISM HAS confirmed that the more vital to society your work is, the less you therefore earn.

Workers the country could not do without such as nurses, truckers and supermarket staff must earn a pittance compared to management consultants and pork futures traders, because that is the way it is.

A Treasury spokesman said: 'As someone who draws a six-figure salary for a job a trained parrot could do, I applaud those in vital roles and regret that they must earn much less.

'Whether you're a binman, a cleaner, a bus driver, a delivery driver, a postman or any of the other people who keep Britain running, your earnings must remain low as our tribute.

'Now is not the time to discuss an increase in salaries. To discuss monetary issues in a cost of living crisis would be vulgar and an insult to the genuine emotion of these people's work. They're missionaries, not mercenaries.

'We couldn't increase their pay without taking away everything that makes them so wonderful. If only I could be like them. But sadly, I have a huge house.'

The spokesman added: 'Our adage is "Keep Calm and Carry On with an Unchanged Economic System". Certainly makes sense to me.'

Are you a posh person

getting pissed?

People get drunk every day, but some of them are posh and so their piss-ups are thrilling, aspirational and news. Are you one of them?

Where are you getting drunk?

A. In your front garden, surrounded by empty cans.

B. In your front garden, surrounded by waiters with flutes of champagne on silver trays.

What's your excuse for getting drunk in a field?

A. Some horses are running fast somewhere nearby and you've put money on one of them.

B. Some horses are running fast somewhere nearby and you own several of them.

What hat are you wearing?

A. A baseball cap bearing the logo of an American sports franchise.

B. A wide-brimmed hat bearing a witty, deconstructed, postmodernist take on baseball caps incorporating cut-up mesh and logos worth £1,200, created by milliner-to-the-stars Philip Treacy.

How are you celebrating passing your exams?

A. Getting hammered, snogging one or more classmates, then waking up the next day and checking out all the photos of it on Instagram.

B. Getting hammered, snogging one or more classmates, then waking up the next day and checking out all the photos of it in the *Daily Telegraph* and on Mail Online.

Drinking and driving is:

A. Not a problem, because you know you can handle it.

B. Not a problem, because you know the chief constable.

How will you end up?

A. A drunken old ruin in a patched leather chair, raging impotently at the modern world after having achieved nothing in your time on this Earth.

B. Same, but in the House of Lords.

How did you score?

Mostly As. You are nothing but a common alcoholic. This country is going to the dogs because of the likes of you.

Mostly Bs. You are effervescent, sparkling, witty and have a column in *Tatler*. Of course it's news when you get drunk – your father owns a county!

You can get pregnant if you share a lane in the swimming pool: myths about comprehensives that grammar school kids believed

DID YOUR parents send you to the nice grammar school? Did the corridors echo with stories about the denizens of the nearby comprehensive? These are the stories you fell for ...

You could get pregnant sharing a lane in the pool

Girls and boys together in the same pool? Wearing nothing but swimming costumes? It all leads to one hideous conclusion: teen pregnancy. Forget everything you know about the practicalities of conception – piss-all, as you spent PSE lessons giggling with your mates – and remember only that sperm are strong swimmers, especially common sperm.

You'd be peer-pressured into drug addiction

Memories of smackhead Zammo on *Grange Hill* were why your parents hot-housed you into passing the 11-plus. So you were well aware that ten minutes with the compo kids and they'd offer a loaded syringe and you'd be too polite to say no. It was disappointing to meet them and discover all they had was nutmeg and dried banana skins.

There were Mars Bar parties at lunchtime

Single-sex grammar school kids never mixed with the opposite gender so believed every lurid tale of wild sexual happenings at the immoral state school. Nobody knew what wild sex involved. Nobody knew what a Mars Bar party was. But you'd all been brought up with Mars Bars as forbidden fruit. If they were just eating them that was dirty enough.

The toilets were haunted

Not in a whimsical *Harry Potter* way, but by a kid who drowned during a particularly forceful swirly by hard bastard fifth years. You still half-believe this and look over your shoulder when you enter the staff loos, even though you have never as an adult met anyone who had their head flushed down a toilet.

You'd get beaten up daily

To your coddled mind, there was no essential difference between a US prison, borstal and a comprehensive in terms of violence. Getting your head kicked in was as normal as double maths. Even the teachers thought nothing of launching a chair across a classroom if someone wasn't paying attention. It meant nothing to the pupils – they were so thick they shrugged it off.

A kid got speared through the neck with a javelin

Grammar schools treat PE like it's a real subject. State schools are more laissez-faire, to the extent that a pupil got speared through the neck during an unsupervised athletics lesson. Debate raged about whether this actually happened or was lifted directly from an episode of *999*, but it seemed plausible that children like that impaled each other for fun.

Rough family throws Gü ramekin away like it's rubbish

A COMMON family has idly disposed of a glass Gü ramekin as if it were nothing more than a wrapper, it has emerged.

The Dawson family ignored all ethical questions surrounding the ramekin and the infinite possibilities of re-use and instead put it straight in the bin after licking out the inside like hungry animals.

Dad Craig said: 'What's the problem? It's not issue one of *Superman*. Yes, it was on the steep side compared to a Müller Corner, but it's hardly irreplaceable.

'What was I meant to do with it, rinse it out and put it in a cupboard? What for? I suppose it'd make a decent ashtray, but you'd be emptying the sodding thing three times a night.

'No, we got rid. In the recycling bin, mind. Chucked it in and it shattered satisfyingly with a lovely tinkle. We all cheered, like the Greeks do after every meal when they smash their plates.

'If you saved them you'd end up with hundreds, all stacked in cupboards, no idea what to do with them but unable to dispose of them in case they might be useful, struggling helplessly on the horns of an ethical quandary. That's no way to live.'

Neighbour Amanda Nash said: 'But what must the men who collect their blue bins think of them?'

Six people you believe yourself superior to who earn three times your income

STILL IMPRESSED with yourself for having a degree, even if it is a 2:1? These six people who you consider yourself above are absolutely coining it:

Train driver, average wage £60,000 pa

How hard can it be? You don't even have to steer. Even in the grubby world of public transport this must be the bottom rung. There aren't even gears to change. But somehow this man in his uniform, doing the job he wanted to do when he was six, is making £60K a year. That's hardly fair.

Binmen, average wage £32,500 pa

Disposing of other people's rubbish is surely lower than a snake's belly in a wagon rut. Anyone with arms and legs could do it, which has to put binmen at the foot of the social hierarchy with barely enough income to live on, right? Unlike your job in media, which doesn't pay enough to clear the interest on your student loans?

Scrap-metal merchant, average wage £34,000 pa

Dirty, nasty work and they're little more than scavengers. You're not telling me that truck's insured. Still, they took your old copper boiler away for nothing, so they're the fools. Later, at a party, you meet the man who owns the scrapyard, and an eight-bedroom Georgian manor house in six acres of land, and a Bentley.

Painter and decorator, average wage £45,500 pa

You'd do it yourself – it's hardly skilled, slapping a coat of paint on – but you're too busy in your office job, so you hire someone. He mentions, while putting up wallpaper, that he usually does major jobs for commercial premises and yeah, sure, we all like to big ourselves up. Wait, his turnover is how much? For a bit of bloody DIY?

Roofers, average wage £66,000 pa

Up scaffolding in all weathers, amusing themselves by wolf-whistling passing women. Scum and dregs of society personified. They charge enough, too, you discover when you need slates replacing. Still, it's hardly work, unlike your prestigious position as a freelance copywriter, living job to job with ten grand on credit cards.

HGV driver, average wage £38,000 pa

No social skills, little formal education and doubtless went to the scummy comprehensive your parents moved house to avoid. GCSE grades negligible. Frankly, if all you can do is drive you've sunk pretty bloody low. Apparently he has a villa in Lanzarote and spends at least three months a year there. What? How? You got six A*s.

Nando's to add viewing gallery

RESTAURANT CHAIN Nando's is to install viewing galleries so those who would never eat there can observe the habits of those that do.

The mid-level balconies will offer a discerning clientele an elevated panorama of diners from young to old and from underclass to Premier League footballers enjoying chicken that is childishly rated according to heat.

Nando's have emphasised that safety concerns are paramount and the galleries will use antibacterial toughened glass capable of repelling thrown food, odours and saliva. The scheme has already been piloted in Nuneaton.

Tilly Cole said: 'It was like a little safari. We sipped champagne and nibbled hors d'oeuvres while observing the less affluent proletariat devour their Peri Peri poultry and their bottomless brown fizz juice.

'It's fascinating how they try to ape an actual fine dining experience without an inkling of understanding. From a distance it even seems quite authentic. Then you see them at the trough, as the audio guide calls it, and realise it couldn't be further removed.

'I would have liked something interactive - perhaps where we could throw chicken from a bucket - but apparently they are aggressive and will nip children.'

Nando's head of marketing Harrison Saunders, said: 'We wanted to expand our customer base, and by offering a physical manifestation of inherent snobbery we've got an entry mechanism for dual-class dining and doubled turnover. All from watching scum.'

Woman claims to be both posh and Welsh

A WORK colleague has made the outrageous claim that she is simultaneously wealthy, privately educated and of Welsh extraction.

Carys Crowther, who is without doubt of a higher social class than all her workmates, has shocked the whole office by asserting that she is Welsh as well.

Jack Green said: 'I thought she meant, you know, of Welsh heritage. Like a Welsh grandmother or something, like you'd have if you played for a Championship team.

'But no. She claims to be actually fully Welsh. Two Welsh parents and born and raised in Wales. How is that possible when she's got a cut-glass accent and an Audi A4?

'Apparently, she grew up in a big house in Penarth, near Cardiff, with six bedrooms and a swimming pool. With no coalmines nearby, not in a valley, and not only her house but the whole neighbourhood was posh. In fucking Wales? Come on.

'It's deeply disorientating. I don't know whether to look down on her or look up to her. All my class instincts are bleeping red and telling me to abort before I make a pass on the basis of false information on her national origin and them all being dirty.'

He added: 'She tried to prove it by speaking Welsh. But any old nonsense could be Welsh.'

Local hard family plans day of low-level troublemaking

A LOCAL hard family has confirmed plans for a day of petty crime and pointless antagonism.

The Potts family lives near Yeovil, where they believe themselves to be widely feared, although most residents simply consider them to be dickheads.

48-year-old Barry Potts said: 'Today I'm going to be driving round in a van, nicking electric fence power packs. They aren't worth much but they're easy to sell - Terry who's got the garden centre near Bath will take them.

'Actually don't say I said that.'

Meanwhile Potts's wife Lindsey is pursuing a bitter feud with her neighbour that possibly started because he had sodium lights on his garden gnomes and they were keeping her awake at night.

Lindsey Potts said: 'I went round and did a shit on his step - it's just what anyone would do in that situation. But I am very reasonable and always ready to bury the hatchet with that twatty little snitch bastard.'

Their daughters, Lisa and Bethany, who are hard-but-popular girls at school, are planning to lock a supply teacher in the stationery cupboard until they cry.

Barry Potts added: 'Do you want to buy a box of 50 windscreen-wiper blades? They're not nicked or anything.'

Low life expectancy versus having to watch *Fleabag*: which is better?

MEMBER OF the underclass? Expected to live 15 to 20 years less than those above you? Is it all worth it if you don't have to watch fucking *Succession*? Find out ...

Underclass: living in persistent poverty with no real hope of escaping it except through violent crime.

Middle class: living at work, with no real hope of escaping it except through watching *Breaking Bad* and *The Sopranos* on a gruelling nightly schedule.

Underclass: often suffering multiple addictions to alcohol, nicotine and a variety of recreational drugs, and consequently unable to maintain employment.

Middle class: no addictions other than vaping, nightly bottle of wine, cocktails at the weekend, occasional weed use and occasional cocaine use, just to be slumped in front of TV.

Underclass: chaotic lifestyles rebounding between family, relatives, partners and prison, constantly finding themselves short of funds and at threat of homelessness.

Middle class: chaotic TV-watching schedules rebounding between Netflix, Amazon Prime, Disney+, Apple TV and Sky, constantly at threat of not having seen the show everyone else is discussing.

Underclass: are not required to pretend any interest in a posh girl with a dysfunctional family and love life hilariously-then-poignantly breaking the fourth wall.

Middle class: are required to pretend they loved every minute of it and found it deeply relatable despite it being as alienating as an arthouse movie about the underclass.

Jesus: toff or chav?

HE WAS a long-haired carpenter, but he preferred wine to lager. The Reverend Dominic Tremain examines the evidence for and against Jesus being a holier-than-thou posho.

Birth

A manger birth isn't fancy and you'd think that would mark him out as a pleb, but back then there was neither NHS nor BUPA so your average maternity hospital wasn't much better than a rickety pub outbuilding surrounded by farm animals. And both parents were present even if Joseph wasn't the actual dad.

Presents

As I say in the pulpit, if you're born on Christmas Day it sucks to be you. But the one person this wasn't true for is Jesus, who invented Christmas and unexpectedly had three blokes turn up with expensive gifts, much like your friend who hits her 30s and suddenly has a hitherto unmentioned uncle who gives her 60 grand for a flat deposit.

Parents

Like a modern alternative family, Jesus had two dads. He became a carpenter like his dad Joseph, making him a very early nepo baby. And his other dad – God – was God. Talk about being given a leg-up from the off. That's opening every door in Galilee, that is.

Hobbies

Jesus was a big fan of fishing, which is one of the few hobbies that appeals to both toffs and chavs. Though there's a big difference between the blokes down the local canal to avoid the wife and Hamish in his tweeds fishing wild salmon in a river owned by an old schoolfriend's whiskey distillery. No information about which one Jesus was.

Food and drink

Jesus loved to throw parties. And not the kind that involve an ounce of skunk, two bags of coke, a Chinese and a FIFA tournament. His had wine, fancy food and a dozen friends chewing over matters theological late into the night. And he once threw an al fresco lunch for 5,000 and handled catering himself, like a Buckingham Palace garden party.

Holidays

They already had the sun, but Jesus went off into the desert for a spiritual retreat for 40 days and 40 nights. Anyone taking six weeks off work to find themselves isn't working on a building site. You'd come back to texts saying you'd been fired but the gaffer is willing to say you're injured if you're claiming benefits.

Politics

Not a fan of money lenders, the Son of God threw a right radge when he came across some of them in a temple one time. While the rich are solidly right-wing supporters of the capitalist financial systems, raised from birth to become bond traders called Toby. Though there are always your Tony Benns.

Clothes

Jesus was a bit of a scruff in his robes and sandals, and there weren't hippies then. Had he been born today, he'd no doubt be wearing Adidas trainers, Puma trackie bottoms and a Superdry jacket.

Verdict: Jesus came from low roots but worked his way up. He might have ended up as la-di-dah as Paul Burrell had he not been nailed to a cross in his early 30s.

Working dog adopted by non-working family

A DOG bred for herding sheep has been adopted by a family bred for working from home on MacBooks.

While grateful for his new home, Border Collie Bobby is unable to comprehend the sedentary lifestyles of his new owners or how they stand them.

He said: 'Tapping away on a flat thing? Talking to a man on a picture? Call that work? I don't.

'I'm used to being active, to running 30 miles a day, to being up at dawn and out in the fields, not 10am starts and vegetating all day waiting for AirPods to charge before I've taken a rigid 10,000 steps according to a fucking Fitbit.

'Instagram isn't work, no matter how many humblebrag photos you post of me wearing poncey hand-knitted jackets in your rustic kitchen. Work's out in a field chasing sheep, not that these layabout wankers would know anything about it.

'Keeping myself busy guarding the house isn't popular either. I pick up that someone - possibly hostile, who might need their throat tearing out - is approaching, warn everyone with a fusillade of barks and it's another bloody parcel. They get eight a day.

'Bunch of workshy bastards. If I could vote, I'd vote Tory.'

Class war begins after toff pushes to front of Greggs queue

THE UK is locked in a bitter and long-awaited class war after a haughty aristocratic man pushed in at the front of a Greggs queue and asked for 'game pie'.

The action scandalised those queuing – a cross-section of society including blue-collar workers, middle-class men slumming it, the underclass and students – and sparked a riot, a lynching and the seizure of a whole town's steak bake supply.

War correspondent Norman Steele said: 'These tensions have been simmering for centuries. That single well-bred arsehole walking into the kitchen of the enemy, with his braying vowels and disregard for social mores, set it off.

'The working classes already occupied all retailers, distribution networks and heavy machinery, so they had an immediate advantage. The middle classes occupied the campuses and office buildings. The upper classes retreated to country estates.

'It's been raging ever since. Snipers in Joseph jumpers. Daring ram-raids by teams of pre-teen twockers. Cavalry wielding polo mallets riding through food courts.

'Checkpoints ask if you've ever had a fish finger sandwich and shoot you for lying. Well-thumbed copies of *Burke's Peerage* are used as hunting guides. Terraced streets are devastated by mocking laughter after a resident pronounces "hors de combat" wrong.

'We estimate it will kill more than half the population of the country and reduce us to medieval conditions. Still, better it's all out in the open.'

Who will win the class war? We assess the forces

THE LONG-GESTATING class war which will slaughter half Britain's population is inevitable and to be relished. But which side has the best chance of victory?

The working classes

Used to manual work, unafraid of death and high in numbers, they have the early advantage. Many have been trained in the use of weaponry, whether in the armed forces or by borrowing Dad's nunchucks from the shed.

At almost half the country, they have the numbers to win. They also have all the vans. But, riven by minor differences of accent, football team and whether the Tories are on their side or not, they also find it impossible to unite or they could have taken over years ago.

The middle classes

They control the media, they occupy the higher ground because it has such a lovely view over the Chilterns but it's a shame about those wind turbines, and they have the degrees. Their children are hale, hearty and know the chemical process required to make napalm.

Unfortunately, they're also averse to any conflict, preferring instead to write passive-aggressive messages on neighbourhood Facebook groups and leave smaller-than-usual tips. When it comes to open warfare this could really hurt them.

The upper classes

Bred for warfare, with centuries of experience climbing on a horse in heavy armour and riding off to battle, the higher echelon of society has grown lazy and decadent. The crusaders' mounts were not trained in dressage, their armour was not owned by English Heritage and their military victories were largely based on sacrificing the lives of others.

However, they may, when tested, find steel at their core, and the world will savour the marvellous sight of Princess Eugenie biting the edge of her shield in a frothing frenzy of bloodlust before decapitating six in a single sweeping blow.

Verdict: stalemate. All sides will be deadlocked and nothing will ever change. This is Britain.

Epilogue:

Book about class enjoyed by middle-class readers

A FUNNY book about social class has been enjoyed so much by its middle-class audience they plan to place it in the downstairs loo, it has emerged.

While the upper classes tend not to read and the working classes demand an exciting plot, publications mocking the mores and sensibilities of the British class system appeal to anxious, insecure, middle-class readers who find comfort in self-mockery.

Professor Felix Lesmoir of the Institute for Studies said: 'The working class and toffs actually get on very well – neither gives a fuck what anyone thinks of them and they enjoy rough sex, albeit not with each other.

'But their real bond is their mutual disdain for the middle class, who are the worst of both worlds: sensitive, delicate fops to those below, illiterate oiks to their betters.

'A satirical book about class is a must for those unfortunates, along with all the other books they feel they should have read, like Piketty's *Capital* and anything by Salman Rushdie. It helps them feel like they would have got into Oxbridge if they'd tried.

'As keen observers of class difference because they're constantly monitoring their place in the hierarchy, they love a bit of satire. It makes them feel they're not wasting their time and it was worth reading the *Observer* all those years so they'd get a joke on *Only Connect*.

'So yes, it's unsurprising that a middle-class man would purchase, read and enjoy a book satirising the class system, chortling heartily and reading bits aloud to his long-suffering wife, who dreams of sex with real men. It's exactly the sort of thing those twats do.'

Contributors

Jonathan K. Bailey

Adam Baird

Chris Ballard

Tom Birts

John Camm

Dom Carter

Angela Channell

Hannah Croft

Karen Dickinson

Poppy Dykes

Bethany Elliott

Liam D. Gillies

Helen Holmes

David Hughes

Matt Hulme

Stanley McHale

Zofia Niemtus

James Pattison

Fiona Pearce

Vicky Richards

Rhiannon Shaw

Christopher Stanners

David Stubbs

Tim Telling

Pete Wallace

Tom Whiteley

Alex Worrall

Three months
of free Mash

FINISHED THIS book and facing months with nothing to read on the toilet? Heart sinking at the thought of a year of bleak, empty, Scandinavian bowel movements?

Subscribe to The Daily Mash instead and the smallest room will echo with hilarity once more. You'll be wiping your eyes more than your arse.

At just £30 per year for unlimited ad-free access, it offers a laugh-per-log ratio that is the envy of publications like the *Financial Times*, *New Scientist* and *Crafty Carper*.

And because you were fortunate enough to buy, or more likely be bought, this book, you can get three months free by entering the code CLASSWAR at:

https://www.thedailymash.co.uk/
subscribe/classwar

Do not share this offer with others. Photocopying this page is strictly prohibited. Everything you have done while reading this book has been filmed and we will not hesitate to put the footage online.